THE
8-Minute
ORGANIZER

THE
8-Minute
ORGANIZER

Easy Solutions to Simplify Your Life in Your Spare Time

REGINA LEEDS

Da Capo
LIFE
LONG

A MEMBER OF THE PERSEUS BOOKS GROUP

Copyright © 2012 by Regina Leeds
Illustrations © Christina Hernandez

Published by Da Capo Press
A Member of the Perseus Books Group
www.dacapopress.com

Library of Congress Cataloging-in-Publication Data
is available for this book.

ISBN 978-0-7382-1571-6 (paperback)
ISBN 978-0-7382-1588-4 (e-Book)

Da Capo Press books are available at special discounts for bulk purchases in the U.S. by corporations, institutions, and other organizations. For more information, please contact the Special Markets Department at the Perseus Books Group, 2300 Chestnut Street, Suite 200, Philadelphia, PA, 19103, or call (800) 810-4145, ext. 5000, or e-mail special.markets@perseusbooks.com

Editorial production by *Marra*thon Production Services.
www.marrathon.net

DESIGN BY JANE RAESE
Text set in 10.5-point Linoletter

First Da Capo Press edition 2012

1 3 5 7 9 10 8 6 4 2

CONTENTS

Introduction   ix

1 Preparing for Change   1

2 Bedroom Minutes   19

3 Kitchen Minutes   47

4 Bathroom Minutes   75

5 Paper Clutter Minutes   93

6 Family Room Minutes   121

7 Kids' Room Minutes   141

8 The Power of Lists   157

9 Maintenance Rituals (and Rewards)   181

Appendix A: Organizing Tools   193

Appendix B: Resources   197

Acknowledgments   205

Index   207

INTRODUCTION

Those who would climb to a lofty height must go by steps,
not leaps.

—ST. GREGORY THE GREAT

You live in a world that feels at times as though it's moving at hyperspeed. Still, you have the best intentions when it comes to making your home a sanctuary, checking items off your to-do list, and creating more "me time." But then the doorbell rings, an instant message dings, the baby cries, your spouse is cranky, your boss needs a transfusion of humanity—all before noon. With more and more demands on our time each day, the goal of an organized home quickly falls by the wayside.

As a result, many of us live in homes that are cluttered and in need of attention. We become exhausted the minute we enter a room and are reminded of all the unmade decisions and unfinished business waiting for our attention. You want to organize your home but feel you don't have enough time. And when you do make the effort, your attempts at organization quickly tumble into chaos. You know exactly how Sisyphus felt with his eternal efforts to roll the same rock up that hill. What's a person to do?

The normal response is the same old, same old. You convince yourself that a kitchen sink looks forlorn without a sky-high pile of dirty dishes. You wonder why you should make the bed when you're just going to tumble into it later. As for those piles that have sprung up on countertops and across the floor like weeds, you decide that they give the space character. But what if you could make *incremental* yet lasting changes in just 8-minute sprints? No, you won't turn into Martha Stewart, but you will get some relief from the demands your environment is making that add to the stress. And over time, your surroundings will be gradually—almost magically—whipped into shape.

Stuff Is Noisy!

Even professional organizers are not immune to the distraction that clutter creates. When I walk into a new client's home for the first time and view the wave of too much stuff, I lose my ability to think clearly. Then, after a few minutes, I remind myself that the whole of any project is overwhelming and the only task at hand is to take incremental steps to the desired end. For example, after I focus on a single stack of papers on a desk rather than the innumerable stacks all over the room—as well as the clothing tossed over the chair, the miscellaneous items stuffed behind the door, the debris on the bookcase, the crowded clusters of plants, and the torrent of personal photos—I'm good to go. I can easily give my client direction because I have no emotional attachment to any of these items. Organizing is in many ways like putting together a three-dimensional puzzle.

But when my clients stand in that same room, they have a different reaction, usually one of guilt or shame. "Why did I let this happen? What's wrong with me? Am I stupid? What must Regina think of me? Why do I have to spend the money to have someone else do this for me?" These comments are the dialogue in their head. Their outside voice usually says, "Tell me, Regina, have you *ever* seen a mess like this before?" I assure them that I have seen scenes like it for over twenty years.

And while all these emotions are roiling, their stuff is talking. No, I don't mean it has a human-like voice that only the dog and I can hear. I mean it seems to emit a frequency that makes clear thinking virtually impossible, and it opens the door to all negative emotions, with guilt leading the parade. Each item has its own particular voice. Every piece of clothing piled on the chair wails that it belongs in a closet. The plants are screaming for water and repotting. Papers are particularly prolific and noisy little creations, reminders of bills that haven't been paid, medical reimbursement forms that haven't been submitted, and little Johnny's homework that hasn't been reviewed.

So how do we quiet the clutter? We clear the debris. We create systems to handle the things we want to keep by giving them a designated place to live. And then we honor what we have created. The process is simple—and this book provides step-by-step instructions, one short project at a time. At first, you may find the process uncomfortable. Change *is* uncomfortable, even when we invite it into our lives. But after a few weeks, you won't be able to remember living any other way.

Zen Organizing

I have a natural gift for creating order out of chaos, but I am also on the spiritual path and deeply interested in the psychological implication of human actions. I need to include these elements in my work with clients, in my seminars, and in my books. This integration of the practical, the spiritual, and the psychological is what Zen organizing is all about. (Stay with me!)

I'm not interested in merely creating a pretty picture in your home. I want your environment to be not only beautiful but functional, so that it *serves* you rather than saps your energy. In turn, you will be free to more easily focus on and achieve success with your life's purpose. Whether you are the president of a large corporation or a stay-at-home mom, I believe your work is important to the forward movement of the planet. Until we respect all work, paths, and contributions without judgment as to their importance, we cannot be whole. If a large orchestra is to perform and one musician elects not to show, the performance will continue but the sound will not be the same. Likewise, if you do not make your personal contribution due to the hindrance of chaos, we suffer as a group. All is not as it was created to be.

People ask me how the term *Zen organizing* came into being. The journey can be described as destiny or serendipity, depending on your view. Many years ago, as I was searching for the title for my first book, I realized that a dramatic shift in energy occurred when an organizing project was complete. Order felt different than chaos. How to elegantly and instantly describe that feeling in a book title eluded me, until a client said, "Oh! You mean it's Zen like!" Westerners have an automatic understanding of the word *Zen* as something peaceful and calm. I had found my word, and in an instant, *The Zen of Organizing* was born.

The Magic Formula

In addition to noticing the change in energy when an assignment was complete, I also realized that I followed the same three steps—eliminate, categorize, and organize—no matter what the project. The types of items in my hands might be different, but the steps I took to achieve success or completion were the same. These steps were so regimented and foolproof that I named them the Magic Formula. To this day, the Magic Formula has been the modus operandi of Zen organizing.

In this book, however, I've added a twist: each task requires only 8 minutes. Longer projects have been divided into 8-minute tasks so you can see progress without getting overwhelmed. Whether the project is a multistep one such as organizing paperwork or the swift clearing out of all dry cleaner bags in your closet, all the projects in this book have been chosen for the good they do on many levels.

Following is a synopsis of the Magic Formula:

- **ELIMINATE:** As we remove from an area what no longer belongs, we begin to exert control. We can see the trees rather than the forest. Eliminate, the first part of the Magic Formula, takes many forms in addition to tossing items in the trash, such as recycling, donating the item, returning (giving the item to its rightful owner), repurposing (moving the item elsewhere in your home), or even regifting (giving an item you've received to someone else). Allow items that have languished in your home unused, unwanted, and certainly unneeded to have a new life with someone else.

- **CATEGORIZE:** The second step in the Magic Formula, categorize, occurs when you assign something to a collection of related items. Common categories include different types of clothing, toys, and food. When you categorize, you have automatic inventory control and can see instantly when you need to replenish an item. What you need is at your fingertips, not the object of a scavenger hunt. A wonderful side benefit to creating categories is that you begin to think in categories about everything, from event planning to work projects.

- **ORGANIZE:** The last step of the Magic Formula is organizing your categories so that your finished project is beautiful, functional, and easy to maintain. Most people think they should begin a project by organizing, but you shouldn't hit the store for hangers, for example, until you know how many and what type you need.

Squandered Time

In my *One Year to . . .* series, I delineate how to organize your home, your work life, and your finances as well as prepare for a new baby. If you have extended periods of time to devote to organizing projects, these books are the most thorough guides in the marketplace.

If you don't have large blocks of time available, you can still achieve an organized life. During the day, you might seek respite from work in a brief phone chat with a loved one, a visit to a favorite social media site, a flip through a magazine, or another cup of coffee. These avenues of relief, however, are temporary. Why not replace them with something that makes your life better now *and* in the long run?

The inherent beauty of the 8-minute organizing project is that it's quick. It relieves congestion in the home or office. It builds your self-esteem as a person who can get and stay organized. And it gives you momentum—you're on to the next thing in a flash.

Following are some examples of the type of people for whom I've written this book. See if you're on my list of those who struggle with being short on time:

- You are busier than ever at your job and find yourself doing the work of many. Your time at home with family and friends is precious, and you resent surrendering a block of time to what you view as another work project. But your time at home will be more nurturing and restorative if you don't have to wage a war just to find a clean towel or batteries for the remote.

- You are out of work and find it difficult to focus on anything but your job search. Depression threatens to knock at your door. An organized environment will make you more productive and happier.
- You are a parent of young children. Children can't understand how much better you will feel after you do the laundry or pay the bills. They need you *now*. Create the order you so desperately need in short bursts of time. In the process, you set a good example for your children.
- You have a physical or an emotional condition. You need the comfort of a calm, organized environment, but you may not have the mental clarity or physical stamina to create what you crave and richly deserve. Working in small bursts of energy and time will not only give you an environment that supports the healing process but also remind you how well you can still function. As I write this, I am just past my ninth anniversary as a cancer survivor. During the months of chemotherapy, I was grateful not only for the support of friends but also for an organized environment. I've walked a mile in your shoes and I promise it's worth the effort.
- You have been diagnosed with ADD or ADHD. Everyone who finds it a challenge to think clearly and to focus can profit from 8-minute accomplishments. Small projects build our self-esteem and assure us that we can succeed.
- You are part of the growing population of aging Americans. Whether you have downsized to a condo, moved in with relatives, or find yourself in a senior center,

you too can enjoy the rewards of 8-minute projects. A nurturing environment knows no age limits but does become more difficult to maintain as we age and lose mental and physical dexterity.

Did you find yourself on this list? If not, perhaps you're wondering whether you should bother to do any of these 8-minute projects. The answer is yes. Where the battle with stuff is concerned, it's always time to enjoy a fresh start.

Found Time

I realize that you are crazy busy, but if you spent a week tracking your time expenditures, you would be amused, amazed, shocked, or surprised at the downtime hidden in your schedule. Perhaps you decide to quickly check your e-mail, only to realize an hour later that you have been sucked into the quicksand of social media. You can find several 8-minute possibilities here! Or maybe you find wonderful release in reading, never bothering to watch the clock. Stop your pursuit a little early and dedicate 8 minutes to making your reading environment more inviting. Have you turned a love of video games into a time-sucking addiction? Steal 8 minutes for your future. The results can only be positive.

We all fritter away time every day. Don't feel guilty: You can't regiment every second without burning out emotionally and physically. You can, however, find small pockets of time that you can redirect to getting organized.

Will finding short bursts of time make a difference? The answer is a resounding "Yes!" You can experience ease in one area of your home or make incremental changes in every room. Whether you tackle one 8-minute project a day, capitalize on your momentum and do three or four 8-minute projects in one session, or engage in multiple 8-minute projects throughout the day, you will effect change. You are in charge of the type of change you want to create and how quickly you want to experience it. Do as much or as little as you want.

How to Use This Book

Peek at the contents, and you can see that the book is organized primarily by room. Within each chapter, I've organized each room by project. I suggest that you quickly read the entire book to get the intention, learn the vocabulary, and decide where you'd like to begin. Then you can follow the book in order or bounce around from room to room and project area to project area. Simply match a project to the needs of your environment, time availability, and mood. You'll find projects that require less than the allotted 8 minutes (called "quickies"), about 8 minutes (the "basic 8's"), and several 8-minute work sessions (labeled "ambitious 8's").

When you get to the last page of this book, I won't tell a soul if you discover that you actually like the process of getting organized and the associated savings in time, money, and energy. Of course, if *you* want to tell the world, I won't argue with you.

I can promise you positive things will happen, but it's up to you to try.

You gain strength, courage and confidence by every experience in which you really stop and look fear in the face. You must do the thing which you think you cannot.

—ELEANOR ROOSEVELT

1

PREPARING FOR CHANGE

Who looks outside, dreams; who looks within, awakens.

—CARL JUNG

Before you can effect lasting change, you need to understand two things: Where did the current mess come from and what would you like to create in its place? The first part of the equation isn't meant to stir up guilt and shame. Rather, if you acknowledge that you created a particular situation, you can see that you can create something else in its place. Put simply, if you can create a messy home, you can create an organized home. I bet you never thought about your situation in those terms, did you?

Open the Door to the Past

The following questions should pique your curiosity about your situation and stimulate your ability to ask yourself the questions that will shed light on your particular mess:

1. What was your childhood home like? Does your current home look remarkably similar? Or have you unconsciously been in rebellion to a tidy mom or dad and the restrictions they put on you?
2. Were either of your parents organized? Did they make it attractive or did their need for order come out of insecurity and a desire to control?
3. Is this the first time you've ever lived with this kind of chaos? If so, was a particular event the trigger? Was a move or a death the culprit? Even good events such as the birth of a baby can unwittingly cause bad changes.
4. When you organize your environment, are you sharing space with someone who will honor your endeavors and give you support? If not, why do you suppose you chose that person? Does being criticized remind you of the way your parents treated you? Does it keep you in a chaotic comfort zone?

You get the idea, right? For more exploration, my *One Year to . . .* series is full of questions that point you to the answers hidden in the past. You can also enlist the help of a friend as long as you ask someone who loves and supports you. In addition, a few sessions with a qualified therapist can often set people on the road to healing.

Determine Where You Are Headed

Before you go out for a walk, get in the car, hop on a bus, or book an airplane ride, you spend some amount of time figuring out where you want to go and how you want to get there. Similarly, when you spend 8 minutes working on a project, I'd like you to remember your destination: why you have chosen to read this book and become organized. Otherwise, the part of you that's afraid of change and likes the security of the status quo will soon go into hyperdrive in an attempt to sabotage your progress! You'll tell yourself that "it doesn't matter if I skip my project," you're "too busy," you'll "get organized later," or you'll "never get this house in order, so what's the point in trying?"

Following are some additional questions, this time about your goals. By answering these questions, you will have the specific information necessary to keep you inspired when the going gets tough.

1. Does your living room or family room habitually look so awful you can't consider having guests over? If the room were neat, tidy, and well organized, would you start entertaining?

2. Are you a good cook? Is it impossible to know or remember because your kitchen cupboards and counters are in an uproar? Have you gained weight or has your blood pressure shot up because of your dependence on fast food? Is it time to start cooking healthy, fresh meals again?

3. Do you think you would sleep more soundly if your bedroom didn't look like a hurricane just blew through? If you're single, is this room's condition part of what keeps you from having a relationship? Would you like one? And if you have a relationship, how does the chaos affect your romantic life? Would you be willing to get organized to help spice up your love life?

4. Are you behind on your bills because you can't seem to remember when they're due? Have friends declared your home office a candidate for an archaeological dig? Wouldn't it be nice to be a fiscally responsible person as a result of a few 8-minute organizing sessions during the next few weeks?

Once again, you see where I'm headed. I want you to know the specific results you seek when you dedicate any 8-minute block of time to creating a new order. This knowledge will help you when you're feeling overwhelmed, distracted, or defeated.

If you are a visual person, you might respond to these questions and then spend 8 minutes daydreaming about the results you seek. How about that for a first assignment: daydreaming! Or you might want to create a dream board or mind map so you can see images of the kind of environment you want to create. All you need are some magazines with great visuals, a glue stick, and some poster board. Before you begin work on your home, work on your dream board or mind map for 8 minutes a day for one week. This exercise is for your eyes only; it isn't an art piece to hang over the fireplace. Have fun. Make discoveries. Don't get stuck in the notion of perfection.

Overcome Difficulties on the Road to Order

Getting organized isn't comparable to rocket science, so why does the task stop so many people in their tracks? You've no doubt uncovered some of your personal reasons after answering the questions presented previously in the chapter, but you may not have considered some other roadblocks. As you read the following mini list, I hope some of you will exclaim, "Wow! I can give myself a break!" Breathe a sigh of relief and realize how much company you have on this journey to a nurturing environment. And rest assured that by dedicating a scant 8 minutes per session, you can make a big difference. Conditions can only imprison us if we allow them to.

1. In the past, have you tried to work on the most challenging areas of your home rather than begin by building a little confidence in the areas you can easily ace? Some of my clients run screaming into the night at the mere mention of tackling paper piles and creating a file system, others break into a sweat when the word *garage* slips from my mouth, and still others tremble when they open their closet door each morning. Start in an easy room and build self-confidence and self-esteem.

2. Are you a master of creating conditions that sabotage your best efforts? Think instead of conditions that will set you up to win.

3. Do you have a chronic physical condition? Or are you undergoing a temporary challenge such as the last trimester of a pregnancy, chemotherapy treatments, or a bruised tendon? Either way, you will tire more easily, both mentally and physically. No wonder you haven't been able to sustain a lengthy organizing project.

4. Are you neglecting your basic health? Honor your body and it will reward you with increased stamina

and the ability to think clearly, two key ingredients for any successful organizing endeavor.

- Your body needs fuel. What kinds of food do you eat? Do you start your day with a good breakfast, or do you skip that meal? What kinds of snacks do you enjoy throughout the day?
- Your body needs sleep. How many hours of sleep do you get each night? Do you sacrifice sleep so you can honor your social media addiction? Your ability to focus will be sharper if you are well rested.
- Your body needs water. How much water do you drink every day? Eight 8-ounce glasses of water is ideal, but this book is about incremental movements forward. Start each morning with 8 ounces of water and increase your intake from there. Water helps you think more clearly, relieves stress, and much more.
- Your body needs exercise. You needn't train for a marathon to gain benefits. Walk 15 minutes a day. Do a few simple yoga postures. Take the stairs instead of the elevator. Exercise clears the mental cobwebs, improves your health, and builds self-esteem. And that's just for starters!

Remember that each of these suggestions makes your life and the process of getting organized easier. If you view them as punishments, you'll be defeated before you begin. Give yourself a break. It's never too late to hit the Stop button on the story you habitually tell yourself and begin a new chapter that finds you the victorious and organized winner you know you can be.

Get Started: Life Tweak

I hope you are fired up and ready to begin. Jump right into completing the projects I have created for you, or ease into the concept of changing the way you function in your environment. If you feel overwhelmed, it's okay to go slowly, but don't stop. The easiest and most powerful way to side-step the urge to quit is to work on creating positive new habits. These *life tweaks* will quickly become part of your daily rituals, replacing less satisfactory actions, and will adjust your current experience for the better. You'll find them in every project chapter.

Actions that keep you organized don't require more time or effort than those that enslave you to chaos. You trade one action for another. The classic example is a simple choice you have every time you enter your home: Will you fling your keys anywhere or carefully place them on a waiting hook or in a designated bowl? The energy expended is the same. The energy saved when it comes time to use the keys again is immeasurable.

My all-time favorite life tweaks follow. You'll find more suggestions in every chapter:

- Make your bed every morning. Time required: 3 to 5 minutes depending on the number of pillows or other decorative items on the bed. (Comforters are much easier to maneuver than the standard bedspread and will save you time.)
- Check all trash cans and recycle containers in the home daily, morning or night, and empty as needed. Time required: 1 minute per can or container.

- Place your keys in the same spot every time you enter your home. If you wear glasses, do the same with them. Time required: negligible.
- Never let dirty dishes pile up in the sink. Handle dirty dishes only once: wash them immediately or rinse them off and pop them in the dishwasher. Time required: 2 to 8 minutes, depending on the number of people contributing to the dirty dish pile!
- Clean dishes should not be allowed to languish on the drainboard or in the dishwasher. Put them away. Time required = 3 to 5 minutes.
- The minute you take off an item of clothing, make a decision about its fate. Does it get rehung in the closet, put into the hamper, or tossed in the bag that goes to the cleaner? Stop leaving clothing on chairs, the bed, or the floor. That action not only delays the decision-making process but also creates a lot of unnecessary visual chaos. Time required: less than 1 minute.
- Complete every action you start. Practice with the physical objects in your home. If you open a cupboard, drawer, or the refrigerator, close it when you have retrieved the item you need. Time required: variable.

Choose two actions that appeal to you and work on turning them into habits. Note that 21 *consecutive* days of repeating an action are required before it becomes a habit.

Mastering these simple actions will not only change your life by making you feel accomplished but also change the way your environment feels. Those with whom you share your space will experience the difference and be invited into the new order of things. This "invitation by example" is more empowering than a family sit-down in which you declare that getting organized will now be everyone's first priority.

For those who are slaves to the past, life tweaks can jump-start your move to a better future. For example, suppose that you grew up in a home with two parents who loved you but were clueless when it came to being organized. You're accustomed to being greeted with the sight of an unmade bed every time you enter your bedroom. But then you start making your bed, and suddenly you are more energized and less prone to depression, and you actually enjoy your bedroom more than you ever have. This new action is suddenly an ingrained part of your everyday routine. One tiny habit has moved you out of your unconscious bondage to the past into a new experience.

Go Beyond: Extra Ammo

It isn't uncommon for my clients to get the "organizing fever." They can't stop when their home is finished, and they start organizing their offices. They may even offer to help family members, coworkers, and friends with their chaos. They finally understand how powerful, rewarding, and life enhancing this organizing business is. For those of you who get the organizing fever while reading this book, I have included at the beginning of each chapter an "Extra Ammo" section that contains some extra action you can take to facilitate the current work. You don't have to embrace these sections, but you'll profit if you at least give them a try.

Make Preparatory Moves

Before you can launch into the projects at the end of a chapter, you frequently need to do a little preparatory work. I tried wherever possible to divide that work into 8-minute segments as well. Think about the ease with which great chefs prepare a tasty meal when their talented and speedy sous chefs have taken the time to chop all the vegetables, cut the meat, and wash the greens. The sous chefs do the grunt work, freeing the chefs to be creative. Preparation is key to success in life, and you'll take advantage of this practice here.

Use Time or Lose It

We think of time as either unlimited or finite depending on our age, our economic status, and the task at hand, but time is actually a commodity like food or money. Time can be squandered or used well but never regained. Those who respond to every e-mail, voice mail, instant message, Facebook post, or tweet immediately often reach the end of the day exhausted rather than accomplished. A common culprit is most likely running the show: low self-esteem or codependency.

One of the main goals of being organized is to lead a self-directed life. I'm not asking you to ignore requests at work, at home, and from friends; I'm suggesting that you prioritize the how and when you get back to people. If you have no time to get organized, to get rest, or to work on what you find important, you may be shocked to discover that everybody else's agenda has become more important to you than your own. Until you learn to prioritize your daily tasks and say no to that which is not key to your goals, you are seeking approval by taking care of the wants and needs of others.

Saying no to an optional commitment that you don't want to make takes only a moment—and can save you hours. However, you will most likely be confronted with an angry chorus of family, friends, and coworkers who are in shock that they now hear the word "no" lovingly but regularly coming out of your mouth. Don't worry! This too shall pass. Those who care about you will adjust quickly. They may even secretly admire you and decide to emulate you. As for the others? Even your mother-in-law and the pest in the next-door cubicle will move on to another victim who will respond to their every whim.

Why do I include this material as part of a book on organizing for what seems like a paltry 8 minutes a day? If you don't become aware of what you habitually do, you will be astonished to find that it becomes almost impossible to find 8 extra minutes a day because your time will be taken up doing things for someone else.

Cultivate the One-Pointed Mind

The "one-pointed mind" sounds quite funny. What does a mind's point look like? A dunce cap, a newly sharpened pencil, or a rocket? This phrase, which comes from Eastern philosophy, is the antidote to multitasking. In simple terms, the one-pointed mind means focusing on one thing at a time. Recent studies show that multitasking is actually counterproductive. Hello? If it were a good thing, we'd all be texting, eating, and making phone calls while driving instead of crashing on the road because it's impossible to focus.

You can perform a simple task to foster the one-pointed mind. Learn how to meditate. Although meditation is an ancient practice from the East that's associated with many spiritual paths, including Buddhism, the Hindu faith, and yoga, you can practice meditation simply to improve concentration and focus. Meditation has countless other benefits, including improved memory, enhanced creativity, deeper sleep, and lower stress-hormone levels. Transcendental meditation (TM) centers abound and are a safe place to learn some basic techniques. Refer to the Resource section for additional online resources where you can learn ancient meditation techniques from a qualified teacher. Add five minutes of mediation to your daily ritual.

If no TM center is nearby, try the following mediation technique, one of many. Focus on the breath. Doesn't that sound easy? Sit in a straight-back chair with your feet flat on the floor. Place your hands on your thighs with your palms facing up. Don't let them touch. (Many people new to meditation find their hands migrating toward each other in their lap. Keep them apart, face up on your thighs.) Close your eyes and pay attention to your breath. Breathe normally. Feel your breath as it enters and then exits your nostrils. Try to do this for five minutes. Think of nothing else but focusing on your breath. When thoughts intrude, *gently* dismiss them, without judgment or annoyance. And don't be surprised if you fall asleep. All of these things are normal in the beginning. Over time, focusing on your breath will get easier. Don't be shocked if you enjoy the practice and the benefits so much that you decide to increase the time you devote to meditation.

Say No to Multitasking

When it comes to multitasking, there's a time to engage in more than one activity and a time to just say no to the madness our society embraces as a sign of productivity. Instead of trying to do two things at once, make use of downtime *between* activities. Suppose you have a dentist appointment at 2 p.m. You're not going to read while the dentist drills, but you could toss your current book or e-reader in your purse in case the dentist is delayed. Or you could send an e-mail or step out of the waiting room to make a short phone call.

On the way home from the dentist, you might make a few calls provided you can do so hands free, it's legal in your state, and the calls are not emotionally charged. This is not the time to call your mother-in-law and do some fact finding on that comment she made over Sunday's dinner. It is a great time to thank a friend for a special gift or favor; while you're stuck in traffic, you'll be flooded with the memory of her kind gesture.

When you get home, you may have to start dinner. During the lull while everything is cooking, why not pay a few bills, pop in a load of laundry, or unload the dishwasher? Many little activities can fill up miscellaneous time. If dinner happens to need only 8 more minutes, you're holding an entire book filled with productive tasks you could accomplish in the meantime.

Before we leave this section, let me ask you a personal question: Who do you think is the sexiest man or woman alive? *People* magazine certainly has some ideas on that that score. Now pretend that your number-one choice is coming to spend the afternoon with you. Whether you lead your guest to your boudoir or to a light lunch in your dining room is something I leave to you. If I were to pop by or send you a text message in the middle of your preparations, I'm betting you wouldn't have time to respond. You'd be focused on this magical afternoon when someone you admire from afar will be all yours for a few hours.

This scenario is a fun way to think about one-pointed focus, isn't it? Try to have this kind of focus as you tackle your chosen 8-minute projects. While doing a project, don't chat with a friend on your cell phone or pause at the computer to view e-mails. You will succeed in direct proportion to the respect you pay your endeavors.

Discover Tricks of the Organizing Trade

Everyone wants to know all the tips and tricks for getting organized. In "Buy It" spotlights in each chapter, I describe my favorite products for the area in question. I highlight ones that have applications in several rooms. That way, if you outgrow one use, you won't be stuck with organizing debris. I also believe in the buying of well-made products. They may cost a bit more upfront, but they more than pay for themselves with their durability and the many ways of service they offer in the home over an extended period of time.

But I have a secret to share with you that may change the way you view the challenge ahead of you. Getting organized isn't about the tools. Showing up for these 8-minute sessions carries the most weight, which is why as a professional organizer I am concerned with sleep, food, water consumption, meditation, and exercise. A person who is chronically sleep deprived, has an unhealthy diet, rarely drinks water, and never meditates or exercises isn't going to be able to make decisions easily. And your stuff comes with such emotional attachment and confusion that thinking clearly is the most valuable tool in your arsenal. Getting organized is ultimately about making decisions about the fate of your stuff.

Make the Most of Your 8 Minutes

Writing a book like this presents a special challenge. I've had to stack the deck with every tool I could think of to make your 8 minutes as productive as possible. And that's why every chapter has two powerful exercises for you to perform before you start your projects: the fresh eyes experiment and the speed elimination. Readers of the *One Year to . . .* series will recognize them immediately. Allow me to introduce them here. The first is quick, fun, and eye opening; the second makes an immediate impact on the environment.

Fresh Eyes Experiment

Do you need a way to get a handle on what needs organizing? Pretend that it's early fall and the television networks are debuting new shows. You've heard a lot about one of them and decide to tune in. The opening scene shows a living room. Without a word being spoken, you suddenly know a great deal about the people who live there. You have a good idea of their socioeconomic status, you can tell whether they have children and pets, and you probably know if their home is a high-rise in Manhattan or a house in the suburbs. You know if they are sloppy or tidy. You might laugh at the chaos or acknowledge that the Zen feel of the home takes your breath away.

That room on television tells you a lot in short order without anyone saying a word. Likewise, your home speaks volumes to everyone who enters. In each chapter's "Fresh Eyes Experiment" section, we're going to figure out what those silent messages are and decide what we would like to broadcast instead.

Speed Elimination

It's a lazy Sunday afternoon. You're on your fifth cup of coffee, the newspaper is spread out all over the floor, and you can't remember if you brushed your teeth. The phone rings. Your mother-in-law is in the neighborhood and would like to drop by to get that pie recipe you promised. You tell her sure, come by in ten minutes. When you hang up the phone, you look around the room. Oh no! What seemed like a cozy room now strikes you as something akin to a horse stall before it gets mucked out. What will your mother-in-law think? You go into high gear. You didn't know you could move this fast! By the time your mother-in-law arrives, your pearly whites are sparkling, the newspaper is in the recycling bin, and the coffee cups are in the sink. You've even fluffed the pillows on the couch.

We have all been propelled into an emergency cleanup mode. And that's how the idea of speed elimination was born. I like to begin each chapter with a speed elimination to make the space feel instantly lighter. Suddenly there's less to clean up, think about, or fret over. The key to successful speed elimination is to shut off your brain and let your gut rule. Make it a game and enjoy the ride. Be sure to set a timer so that you don't get lost in the debris, your thoughts, or unwanted emotions. Use a kitchen timer or the one on your cell phone.

In Conclusion

The most frequent lament I hear goes something like this: "Regina, I get organized all the time. Two weeks later, the house is back to being a mess. What should I do?" If you, too, think that even your 8-minute projects are destined for failure, remember that you have probably been tidying up, not getting organized. When things are stashed behind doors, stuffed into closets and drawers, and hidden in nooks and crannies, the visual scene is calm but deceiving. The order created isn't real. After a home is organized, every item has a specific place. When you restore order, you don't hide items; you take them home. A blueprint, not a chance whirlwind, is in charge. A Zen organized space with established systems and designated areas for all possessions is a very different experience, one I know you will enjoy.

It's time to begin. As mentioned, I suggest that you read the book through once before you dive in and choose your first project. Then do one project a day, schedule several 8-minute sessions throughout the day, or go crazy and string several sessions together. (One caveat: Complete a multistep project in consecutive 8-minute sessions before you move on to a new project. Being surrounded by several in-progress projects will only make you crazy.)

My goal is to help you experience glimpses of a Zen organized life by working in short bursts of time and energy. Let's get started, shall we?

2
BEDROOM MINUTES

Where there is great love there are always miracles.
—WILLA CATHER

We've established that the space you call home should nurture you and make life easier—just walking in the front door should bring relief. But life, especially when it involves sharing space with others, is often stressful. At these times, you should be able to retreat to the private sanctuary known as your bedroom. Or would you call your bedroom a disaster area?

Often the smallest change will make a huge difference in how we feel in this room. The short projects in this chapter are designed to relieve congestion so that the room itself invites you in to relax, whether that relaxation involves comforting a baby, embracing your lover, or taking a nap.

Life Tweak

Make your bed every day. The process doesn't have to be complicated—you don't need military corners or a pile of decorative pillows. With the top sheet tucked securely at the foot of the bed, simply smooth the sheet into place in the morning. Straighten the comforter and fluff the pillows. Just 2 minutes and you're done! Keep it simple, and making your bed will soon become a habit.

Extra Ammo

My clients always want guidelines and rules for eliminating clothing from their closets. I find rules arbitrary: "If you haven't worn it in 6 months (or a year), you should give it away." "When you buy something new, you need to get rid of something else." If these rules work for you, by all means use them. But I'm more interested in the emotional attachment that makes you hesitate to part with a garment you no longer wear. Following are examples of internal dialogues you might conduct when you can't make an immediate decision about an item. Do any of these unlock the real hold the article has over you?

- My (late) father (mother, friend) bought this for me.
- My ex got this for me on that romantic trip we made last year.
- I might need this one day.
- I have never worn this and feel guilty every time I look at it.

- I paid good money for this and it might come back in style someday.

Your attachment is usually about guilt or fear and has little or nothing to do with the actual item. The big fear underlying all of the preceding statements is this: Will I be making a mistake if I eliminate this item? Free the space in your closets and drawers and you'll free a space in your life for more and better to come to you. Right now, your life is getting a busy signal.

Fresh Eyes Exercise: The Bedroom

Spend 8 invaluable minutes in your bedroom taking stock of the situation. Pretend this bedroom belongs to someone else. What do you see? Is the closet bulging with clothing? Does your nightstand hold enough books to make the local library jealous? Is the floor covered with the inventory of Toys 'R' Us or Petco?

What about items that belong in other rooms? Plates, bowls, coffee cups, and the like. Do you habitually let these items stack up before you return them to the kitchen?

List everything that prevents this room from being called serene. I bet your list indicates that most items have no designated home. Orphans are crowding your space. You need to find them their "forever homes."

While you're gazing with fresh eyes at this room, note some bigger projects that you could tend to in the future. These tasks, which take a lot more than 8 minutes, would improve the room's makeup. For example, does the room need a fresh coat of paint, updated window treatments, new bedding from sheets to duvet cover, a sanded floor or a clean carpet? Schedule these big-ticket items on your calendar. Writing down what needs to be done—even if the date is six months from now—moves the project from wishful thinking to concrete goal.

You shouldn't make judgments about the state of this room. You are simply an impartial witness to the current state of affairs. When you can delineate the problem, it becomes less overwhelming. You're moving from "I hate my bedroom" to "I have a list of things I can do to make my bedroom more like a sanctuary." Don't dwell on this exercise; an 8-minute session should suffice.

Speed Elimination: The Bedroom

Many of our 8-minute projects involve eliminating after carefully considering an item's meaning, usefulness, and condition. But for now, I'd like you to spend a wild but concentrated 8 minutes moving rapidly in the bedroom— and closets—eliminating anything destined for the trash or for recycling. Also grab items that belong to others or need to be returned to the store. Have a trash bag and a bag or sturdy box for recyclables at the ready. If you have a lot of returns (to others or to the store), have a box for them too. This isn't a thinking exercise, so don't ponder the pros and cons of tossing an item. You're looking for the no-brainers.

Exercise your "trash muscle." If you have difficulty eliminating anything from your life, take heart. Getting rid of things you don't need, don't want, or won't ever use requires muscle (your "trash muscle," that is), and you need to strengthen it over time.

Begin today with 8 dedicated, focused, speedy minutes! Set your timer. Shut off your emotions, turn on your rational brain, and start eliminating. When the timer announces the end of the exercise, take out the trash and the recycling immediately. Don't let these items loiter in the space. And be sure to return those items that have been lingering in your environment. They want to go home. Take care of the ones migrating elsewhere in your home now and schedule the store or friend returns over the next week.

8 Minutes to Sanctuary

QUICKIES

If you limit yourself to the quickies in this book and do nothing else, you will make an impressive difference in your environment. Quickies are meant to be effective and fun and to take almost no time. Closet quickies are some of my favorites!

Banish Dry Cleaner Plastic

Often clients will leave the bedroom for a few minutes to get us some refreshments or to answer the phone. When they return, they are shocked to see that a lot of space suddenly exists in a closet that was bursting just a few minutes before. Because they're terrified that I have tossed some items without checking with them (something I *never* do), I share with them my secret space-making tip: Toss the plastic bags your dry cleaner sent home with you. And that is your first quickie! Dispose of the bags responsibly; you don't want a child or an animal to get hold of them and suffocate.

These bags do more than take up valuable space. If you leave a piece of clothing covered in plastic for several weeks, the cleaning agents become sealed in the fabric. When you finally wear the item, you will be breathing in those cleaning agents. Remove the plastic and air out your clothing.

BUY IT: A COTTON COVER

For items that must be covered for a long time, use cotton covers, which keep clothing clean while allowing the fabric to breathe. You can purchase covers for individual garments or multiple ones. Ladies with busy social lives often place their cocktail dresses in one of these canvas holders. You can find an assortment of canvas covers at The Container Store.

Escort Wire Hangers Out the Door

After you've pulled off those plastic covers, see how many empty wire hangers you can eliminate from your closet. Empty wire hangers are an unnecessary item that eats up valuable space. Moreover, wire hangers are the worst choice for your clothes because they can leave black marks or shoulder bumps and over time will literally destroy fabric. Remember, a wire hanger is a means of transporting your newly cleaned and pressed garments, not a permanent perch for them! Recycle or return those wire hangers to your dry cleaner.

BUY IT: NEW HANGERS

So what are the best hangers to use? It all depends on the size of your closet and the number of garments you need to hang. I prefer wood hangers and use them almost exclusively. They add a rich look to the closet and preserve the integrity of the clothing. My second choice is the new, thinner hanger that is coated so that garments won't slide off. (Sold under names such as Huggable, Slim Grip, or Velvet Finish.) Don't fret: The coating won't come off on your clothing.

You needn't break the bank and purchase all the hangers you need at once. You can spread out your purchases over time. When a relative or friend asks what you want for your birthday or Christmas, just smile and say, "Why hangers and canvas covers, please!"

A word to the wise: Switching out hangers is labor intensive. If you purchase all new hangers, take advantage of 8-minute work sessions and do the switch gradually. Be sure to enjoy the changing visual as you go from wire to wood or whatever hanger type you choose. If you have teenagers in your home who would like to earn some extra cash, hire them to switch out your hangers.

Unhamper Your Style

The hamper is a necessary but pesky item. Take a moment to evaluate yours. Is it too big and robbing you of space, or too small with clothing erupting between visits to the laundry? Does it clash with the décor? Is it placed correctly? Sometimes an attractive hamper can blend into the décor of a bedroom rather than be stuffed into the closet. Spend a few minutes shopping at your favorite online home stores to see who has the hamper of your dreams. If you intend to stick your hamper in the closet, think utilitarian and save money. Plastic hampers sell for a few dollars. If you need your hamper to become part of the décor, consider a more attractive material such as wicker.

Get Trashy

Do you have a trashcan in the room? If not, you should! Again, check online for a trashcan that fits the décor, or see whether you can repurpose a trashcan from another room. You may be able to find a wicker trash can that works perfectly with your new wicker hamper.

Or if you find you have an extra, tall can, pop it into the entry closet and stash your umbrellas there. When you think creatively, you can find all sorts of uses for your organizing tools.

Let in the Light

On a hectic morning, can you tell your dark blue socks from the black ones? Do your lamps need bigger bulbs? Or is the overhead lighting so harsh that it makes you feel like you're in a prison holding cell? Take a few minutes to consider your lighting. If you don't have a stash of lightbulbs on hand, schedule a trip to the store so you can stock up. Something as simple as changing a lightbulb can instantly change how you feel in your space.

8 Minutes to Sanctuary

BASIC 8'S

You'll need a full 8 minutes for these projects, but with your newfound organizing self-esteem on the rise, I think you'll be eager to accept the challenge. These projects make a more dramatic impact on the environment than the quickies.

Line Up Your Handbags

Instead of letting your handbags pile up in a heap, why not stuff them with tissue paper and line them up in color order? You can use any color sequence that pleases you. I use white and off white; beige and brown; blue and purple; pink and red; green and yellow; and grey and black.

Over the years, I've discovered that my clients love the look of a purse plumped-up with tissue paper, but they don't want to deal with rumpled paper every time they use the purse. Here's a fix: Put the tissue paper in a plastic zippered storage bag from your kitchen, so you can move the paper in and out of your purse with ease. When you want to use a purse, fill its spot on the shelf with the purse's bag of tissue paper.

Tissue paper tends to come into our lives in purchases we make in department stores or in gifts we receive for our birthday or holidays, so now you have a great way to reuse it. If you need a lot of tissue paper, don't buy it at a card store; instead, check out a big box store such as Costco.

Gather Stray Garments

What do I mean by stray garments? Do you have orphan items tossed on your chair or bed? Hang them up. Spend 8 minutes dealing with these items, deciding whether they're candidates for a hanger, the laundry, the dry cleaning, the donation bag, or the trash. As the garments start to vanish, that overwhelming feeling will be replaced by a feeling of control. Just think how easy it will be to get into bed this evening or how lovely it will be able to actually sit on your chair and relax.

Shelve Books

I love books and think reading is one of life's great pleasures. But often the sheer volume of books can threaten to destroy the order in a room. Do you have stacks all over the floor and more stacks on your nightstand? It's time to get some control so that reading can once again be a pleasure. Take 8 minutes to gather your scattered reading material and return it to your bookshelves. (Avid readers need a bookcase in this room to avoid unruly stacks.) Toss outdated magazines.

When you finish, you will be left with an attractive and organized reading area. And you will no longer need to pole-vault over stacks of books or magazines just to reach your partner or your pillow.

BUY IT: A SMALL BOOKCASE

If books tend to take over your bedroom, the easiest solution is to acquire a simple bookcase specifically for this room. You can find a small bookcase at your local home store or secondhand store, Ikea, or The Container Store. You might even have one in another room that would work here.

Declutter an Overstocked Shelf

Pity the poor closet shelf. It usually has clothing piled high in stacks that tumble into each other with amazing regularity. What's a shelf to do? Well, if your shelf could speak, the first thing it would ask is that you divest yourself of some of the items on it.

During your initial 8 minutes of clutter clearing and organizing, deal with each item on each shelf. (If you have a large walk-in closet, give yourself 8 minutes per shelf or zone.) Ask yourself whether you need the item. If you do, create a category for it, such as handbags or sweaters. If the item belongs in another room, put it in a separate pile. If you don't need the item, decide whether you want to donate or toss it. The goal is to whittle your categories to the precious few items that will indeed be worn or used.

BUY IT: A CLOSET SHELF

Most closets have one shelf, with a cavernous space between it and the ceiling. Why not install an additional shelf? Simply install a wood bracket on each side and place a piece of wood across. This second shelf might provide the space for storing out-of-season clothing, keeping the existing shelf for the current season. See if you have the room, and then break out the toolbox.

Choose a Sweater Solution

Storing sweaters is difficult: They tumble, snag, and merge into unmanageable piles. Fortunately, you can store and retrieve sweaters in many ways. In this section, I outline the most popular methods. Feel free to employ more than one solution:

- Arrange your sweaters by color on a shelf, so they're easy to see and grab. Separate the stacks with shelf dividers. These handy tools are inexpensive and useful wherever you have categories, such as the pantry and the linen closet.

- Use a cardboard lifter to keep your stacks neat. Get a piece of sturdy, 8½-×-11 piece of cardboard with smooth edges. Then, when you want to wear a particular sweater, slide the cardboard under the next-higher sweater and lift up. Now you are free to remove the one you need without disturbing the others.

- Buy canvas storage bags with zipper closures. Each bag holds two or three sweaters depending on their weight. They work well on a shelf, organized by sweater type (cardigan versus turtleneck, for example) or color.

- Create a stack of large acrylic drawers, if you have extra floor space. This solution also protects your sweaters from dust.

- Use an acrylic drawer on a shelf. This solution might work for tall people, but those of average height would need a step stool. Consider how you will use something before you decide where to place it.

- Keep your sweaters in a spare dresser drawer.

BUY IT: A LAUNDRY FOLDER

If you aren't skilled at folding clothes, you can purchase a Flip-FOLD laundry folder at The Container Store. This device takes the guesswork out of uniform folding and makes your sweater stacks look like those in a boutique on Madison Avenue!

Preserve Your Sweaters

Moths feast on wool and cashmere, destroying your precious collection of sweaters. But I don't use mothballs because of their smell. If you seal a sweater in a bag with mothballs, you may preserve the sweater for next season, but will you be able to stand that smell when it comes time to wear the sweater? Use cedar instead: It's effective and humans find the odor appealing rather than repelling. You can also buy or make sachets of cheesecloth filled with dried lavender or mint or even canned tobacco. (Dried tobacco won't make your clothes smell like a cigarette. You have to light up and puff away in your closet to get that effect.)

Clear the Bedroom Floor

Children and pets have toys. They come with the territory. And the territory they invade is frequently mom and dad's bedroom. Where these toys are permanently stored and how many we purchase varies with each person. Some parents love toys scattered about the room, while others feel that the toy a child entered the room with should be the toy the child exits with a few minutes later. They apply these same rules to Fido and his bones and squeaky toys. The choice is yours and will reflect many things, not the least of which is how you feel about this room and how you intend to use it.

I suggest that you use a container to catch the toys so the floor doesn't look like an aisle explosion at Toys 'R' Us on sale day. The bedroom is meant for play and rest. You and your spouse aren't going to be feeling frisky if you have to tip-toe over Legos and toss a few teddy bears off the bed in a moment of passion. You probably have a basket in another room that will do the trick nicely and add to the ambience in this room.

Set a timer for 8 minutes and follow these steps:

1. Scan the floor for items that can be thrown in the trash. Immediately toss these items into a garbage bag.
2. Set aside items that belong elsewhere in the home, such as abandoned coffee cups or DVDs from the family room. Keep items sorted by room to facilitate the return process.
3. Gather all toys and sort by type: stuffed animals versus games or books versus Barbie dolls.
4. Bag any items destined for the trash or the charity donation box. Set aside toys that need to be returned to another location such as the family room or your child's bedroom.
5. Place clothing in the hamper, the dry cleaning bag, or the closet, depending on its condition.
6. Return shoes to the closet.

Your 8 minutes should be up right about now. Return the items that belong elsewhere in your home or apartment. Toss the trash if it's full. If you don't have a container or designated area for the toys, you can always use a cardboard box as a *temporary* fix and put one on your shopping list. Admire your handiwork and pat yourself on the back. Doesn't the floor look great?

If you have a particularly messy floor, don't become overwhelmed or demoralized by doing every category of item at once. For example, you might first spend 8 minutes sorting toys. Then devote 8 minutes to the clothing that litters the floor, and wrap up the process by giving Fido's rope toys, pig's ears, and bully sticks their own block of time. The key with any of these projects is to make incremental progress, honor what you accomplish, and never give up.

Assess the Battle of the Nightstands

Whenever I walk into a client or friend's bedroom for the first time, I check out the setup on both sides of the bed. Are there two nightstands? Are they equal in the space and storage they provide? If this is a partnership, are the tools of the bedroom such as the phone, the light, and the TV remote on one side of the bed? If so, this setup may indicate a power imbalance in the relationship. Assess the situation in your setup: Does one person have all the power or all the mess? You may discover that you need a different size night table, a second table, or perhaps a new lamp. You may feel it's time to have a talk about the division of those bedroom tools.

Clean Out the Nightstand Drawers

After your investigation in the preceding section, dedicate 8 minutes to a speed elimination of items clearly earmarked for the trash or another location in your home. Nightstand drawers are frequently filled with expired medications, loose change, extra remotes, and enough pens and pencils to keep a large corporation happy. Be realistic: What do you need before bed or in the middle of the night? Keep this area lean and clean.

Clean out your drawers and decide what organizing tools will best house the items you elect to keep near you. (If another person is involved, be sure to secure permission to deal with his or her possessions before you organize the other nightstand.) Small clear acrylic drawer organizers work wonders here. And drawer liners are a nice finishing touch because they hold everything in place—you don't want your beautiful design to go flying the first time you shut the drawer. If you have empty jewelry boxes, you might use the boxes and their lids to keep things tidy until you get formal drawer organizers.

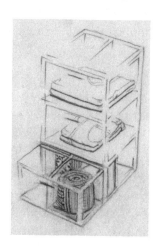

8 Minutes to Sanctuary

AMBITIOUS 8'S

There's no denying that some key projects in the home can't be completed in 8 minutes, but that doesn't mean they should be avoided. I get around the problem by dividing each project into segments that last roughly 8 minutes. Don't let too much time elapse before you complete your entire project.

Ease Crowded Dresser Drawers

Most people stuff everything but the kitchen sink into their dresser drawers. Garments come out wrinkled and you look rumpled if you don't take the time to iron them. For this project, devote 8 minutes to each dresser drawer. Some drawers will go quickly, so keep track of the minutes you save and tack them onto the time it takes to complete more difficult drawers. Follow these steps:

1. Eliminate whatever is tattered, full of holes, or permanently stained. Discard, too, any item that is simply out of step with current fashion. We all purchase super-trendy garments from time to time and later wonder, "What the heck was I thinking?" whenever we see them in the drawer. Let them go.
2. Set aside the items for donation. You'll be grateful for the tax deduction at year's end.
3. Find items to hang in your closet instead of folding in a drawer. Some clients wouldn't consider putting jeans in a drawer; others think putting jeans on hangers takes up too much room in a closet. Make your decision based on the number of items in a category and the space you have.
4. Decide how you want to store your socks: rolled or folded in half. Many people roll their socks and fold the top over the ball to keep the pair intact. You can do that with your big, thick sport socks if you want,

but I would avoid this technique when storing good socks because it stretches the fabric.

BUY IT: A SOCK ORGANIZER

I use sock organizers in my drawers. The plastic variety is inexpensive and keeps the socks sorted and in one place. You get more space in your drawers when small items aren't free-floating. I use containers for underwear and bras as well.

Have you dedicated an entire drawer to your collection of white exercise socks? If you have shelf or floor space in your closet, I suggest that you put your socks in a container here to free up the dresser. Purchase a basket with a liner (to prevent snags) or an acrylic drawer, which has the added benefit of keeping them dust free. Or stack a few drawers in your closet and create an instant minidresser.

Thin Out the Closet

We all make clothing mistakes, don't we? And our blunders hang in our closets for years, taunting us with guilt every time we open the door. Set a timer for 8 minutes and move like your hair is on fire! No time for dwelling, sentimental stories, and guilt. From hangers and shelves, pull garments you have never worn or no longer wear. Let your gut be your guide.

Before you start, however, get three containers (sturdy garbage bags or cardboard boxes) to catch your former treasures: one for trash, another for donations, and a third for the occasional item earmarked for a friend or family member. (Note: If the last container is the largest group, you're cheating. Cousin Mary may love you dearly, but she doesn't want all your fashion faux pas taking up room in her closet. Give them to charity.) Get these items out of the house today so that you don't backslide and put items back in the closet.

Group Clothing by Type
Now that your closet has been thinned out, you are surely saving time getting dressed each morning. Want to save even more time? Take 8 minutes and regroup your clothes in sections by type (blouses, shirts, suits, jeans, and so on).

Rearrange Clothing by Color
In the last project, you organized your clothes by type to save time getting dressed. Here, you save even more time by arranging each type according to color. Here (again) is the color order I use: white and off white; beige and brown; blue and purple; pink and red; green and yellow, and grey and black. When you finish, you will be so comforted by the visual that you will enjoy getting dressed. You'll also have more fun with clothing in general. Soon your daughter may not be the only fashionista in the house!

Shuffle Shoes
Imelda Marcos, the wife of the former president of the Philippines, was famous for her shoe collection. At the height of her collecting, she was reported to own several *thousand* pairs. Did you hear that, Kardashian sisters? With any luck, you have fewer pairs, and now the task at hand seems easy, doesn't it? In this section, I break down the work you need to do on your shoe collection into a series of 8-minute rounds. You can spread them out over

time or knock them out in one day, according to the size of your collection and the depth of your attachment.

Round One
Write down the types, or categories, of shoes you own. Your list might look something like this: work, play, sandals, evening/cocktail, and hiking. Now consider each type in turn. Does it have to live in your master bedroom closet? Or could it be housed in some other closet, freeing up space in this one?

Round Two
Pull all your shoes out of the closet. (Aren't you delighted you cleared some floor space?) Instead of bringing them out in one messy pile, separate them by the categories you listed in round one.

Round Three
Speed-eliminate in each category. Eliminate as many shoes as you can, especially the ones you haven't worn in ages—work quickly and ruthlessly! Your local charity will be grateful for your generosity and your closet will heave a sigh of relief. Are any of the shoes you intend to keep in need of repair? Set those aside to be dropped off at the shoe repair shop. Depending on the size of your shoe collection, you may be able to eliminate in one 8-minute round or in 8 minutes per category.

Round Four
Now that you have whittled down each category, you need to return them to the closet in an organized fashion. In

this round, choose a storage solution. Shoes scattered about the closet floor are destined to look messy, get separated or lost, and drive you insane.

You won't be surprised to learn that no matter which organizing solutions you choose, I suggest keeping the shoes in color and height order (start each color with flats and move up to the highest heels). Having all your shoes at your fingertips will save you not only minutes getting dressed but also money. The next time you feel you need a pair of summer sandals, you'll be able to see at a glance the 12 pairs you already have in your closet.

BUY IT: A SHOE RACK

A good shoe rack is essential. Most are stackable, so you can put in the number of shelves you need. I prefer flat wooden shelves because they hold everything from heels to flats with ease. Another great but more expensive choice is to use acrylic shoe drawers in a stack. They keep your collection visible and clean. The large-size shoe drawer handles just about any size shoe or heel height. Please note I said shoe *drawer*, not box. If you have a stack of shoes and need the one on the bottom, a drawer is easy to open; lifting a stack of shoe boxes is a pain in the neck. You can use shoe drawers just for your evening shoes and keep them tucked away on a shelf or in a stack in the back of the closet.

Exercise and play shoes take up a lot of space and people tend to have multiple pairs for different activities. An over-the-door canvas shoe bag is ideal for these types of shoes. Use the lower pouches to store flip-flops and summer sandals.

Explore under the Bed

Remember in the Introduction when I said stuff was "noisy"? Well, it's time to devote a few minutes to what's dancing, singing, and jiving under your bed! Are you sleeping over outgrown baby clothes or holiday decorations? Have you stored photograph albums, old love letters, or even camping equipment under the bed? Whatever is hidden there, let me ask you this: Do you sleep well in this room? Chances are the stuff is interrupting your rest at night.

Wouldn't you like to have clear space if only to be able to get the vacuum cleaner under there? And we won't talk about the invitation to critters that cardboard boxes and other storage materials represent.

Round One

Now that I've scared you, let's set aside 8 minutes for an archaeological dig. What the heck *is* under your bed? If the area is packed, do one side at a time. And if it's *really* bad under there, divide each side in half, for a total of four 8-minute work sessions. As you unearth each item, ask yourself whether you really need it. Make a pile of items you can toss or donate.

Round Two

Now ask yourself whether under the bed is the best place to store each item that remains. You may discover that some items can now live elsewhere in the home. If your children have grown up and live in their own homes, you could store things in their old room, either in the closet or under the bed. What about the entry closet or the garage? We don't need to stay rooted to one spot forever and neither do our possessions.

Round Three
If you decide that some or most items must be kept under the bed, ask yourself if they are stored in the best way possible. You'll find low, flat plastic containers made for this space. My favorite are on wheels, which makes the items more accessible. If your bed is built on a platform with drawers, store each item neatly. Every area of your home should support you rather than fight, antagonize, or annoy you. If clothing presents no emotional ties for you, the time you spend working in the bed drawers will be minimal.

Corral Costume Jewelry
In most homes, the bedroom dresser's top drawer is chock full of costume jewelry and the top of the dresser hosts an overflowing jewelry box. Often, however, we wear the same pieces every day and our collection is left unused and so tangled that you couldn't wear the items even if you wanted to!

Round One
Spend your first 8 minutes getting the lay of the land:

- Is all your jewelry in this room? If not, could it be gathered in one place?
- Is your good jewelry mixed in with your costume pieces? If possible, keep your good jewelry in a secure

location, such as a home safe or a locked jewelry drawer, and place your costume jewelry in an immediately accessible area.

- Do you traditionally wear certain pieces every day? If so, could those pieces be kept separate?

Round Two

The next 8-minute project will be daunting for some of you. Before you begin cleaning out anything, think about your costume pieces. Do you almost never wear certain pieces? One of the universal pleasures all little girls have is playing with jewelry. Do you have or know a child who would treasure and enjoy some of the items you have languishing in this drawer? If you don't know anyone personally, would you be comfortable donating some of this jewelry to a charity or a local community theater? Costume jewelry tends to overtake valuable drawer space and is rarely worn. Consider the possibility of allowing your collection to go from one that's full of items you get some pleasure looking at to one that's smaller but actually used.

Round Three

Before you tackle the contents of the drawer and jewelry box, take another session to consider whether you're storing items in the most space-efficient manner. Ordinary jewelry boxes that the local department store gives you with a purchase work well in a shallow dresser drawer. I like open boxes so I can see everything at a glance. If you don't have enough boxes, use the lids separately. In 8 minutes, the average collection can be whipped into shape.

If you have a larger collection, you may need additional solutions. Consider the following:

- A traditional jewelry box is a nice way to store your better pieces. And if the box is attractive, you have a nice decorative item added to the room's basic décor.
- Do you have any wall space in your closet? Often the wall straight back in a walk-in closet is blank. You can put up a few squares of cork and hang your longer pieces and bracelets on hooks.
- Some inexpensive acrylic jewelry containers can hold hanging jewelry, so your necklaces stay untangled and ready to wear. You'll need space on the top of a dresser for this solution. (By the way, if you have a walk-in closet, does it have room for your dresser? Moving the dresser to the closet provides more floor space in the bedroom.)
- Expensive jewelry or family heirlooms should be placed in a safety deposit box or a home safe. A word to the wise: If you can pick up your safe, so can a thief, so invest in a secure safe. And remember to ask your insurance agent if you need a jewelry rider on your homeowner or renter's insurance policy.

After you look at your pieces and your room and decide how you are going to proceed, your final 8-minute project may be delayed while you shop for a jewelry box, some cork, and an acrylic container or two.

Round Four
Transfer your jewelry to its new home.

Your New Bedroom Exit Ritual

Now that your bedroom is exuding some peace and calm, you'll want to preserve the new order. In this section, I provide some quick tasks to perform each morning as you leave for the day and each night as you prepare for sleep.

I can hear some of you before I get to the first tasks. "But Regina, I'm too busy to add more tasks to my day!" I understand your concern. But here's a big organizing secret: Getting organized doesn't take more energy or time than staying stuck in chaos. You are merely redirecting the same energy. For example, it takes 2 minutes to make a bed. Meanwhile, if you leave your bed disheveled, you may lose things in the bedding and waste time searching for them. The bed becomes a magnet for laundry. In addition, every time you see the unmade bed during the day you will feel sleepy. Everything you do becomes more difficult, as you will be focused on how great a quick nap would be.

Following are my suggestions for your new bedroom exit and entry rituals:

- Make the bed.
- Put clothing in your closet, hamper, or dry cleaner bag—these are the only three options! Never toss garments on the floor, drape them over a chair, or leave them on your bed.
- Place shoes in the shoe rack.
- Return miscellaneous paraphernalia (from Junior's toys to your books) to their designated spots.

- Return dirty dishes, glasses, and all food items to the kitchen.
- Turn off the lights.

Both order and chaos are created by dedication to the steps that create them. Change your focus from confusion to calm, and your actions will follow. The result will be a place of peace waiting to nurture you whenever the stresses and strains of daily life threaten to overwhelm you.

A Bedroom Sanctuary

As you complete the projects in this chapter, your environment will become calmer and more peaceful. The energy of a space exerts an unspoken influence on everyone who enters. If the kids seem less stressed and your spouse is more loving, I wouldn't be surprised. Something about saving time and emotional energy makes a body happy.

KITCHEN MINUTES

The word impossible *is only in the mind and not in the heart.*
—SRI CHINMOY

Hands down, the most popular room in the home is the kitchen. Throw a party and where will you find most people? In the kitchen, even if it's as tiny as a postage stamp. This room is inherently nurturing but also, sadly, usually in upheaval. In my twenty-plus years as a professional organizer, I've rarely seen a kitchen that was well organized.

I trace the origins of this chaos back to moving day, when everyone is trying to get boxes off the truck and empty them as quickly as possible. In an effort to be helpful, Aunt Ethel or your best friend Zelda toss items into cupboards with great abandon. "I emptied the boxes, sweetheart. You can organize it all later." As we used to say in Brooklyn: Fat chance! If you can find the coffee pot on the first morning, life takes off with no looking back. But this plan invites waste: Time is squandered looking for items; food spoils; pests may even appear.

Most kitchens are disorganized simply because no one focused on organizing them. This wonderful room offers an array of 8-minute projects and is ripe for chores. What child can't learn how to set and clear the table, wash dishes or load the dishwasher, take out the trash, or polish the silverware for the holidays? When in doubt, delegate.

Life Tweak

If decisions are the fuel driving the organizing train, another secret ingredient makes that train go even faster: completion. No place is better than the kitchen for cultivating this habit. What do I mean by completion? Here are examples of its opposite. When some people need a dish and a glass, they open the appropriate cupboard doors but never close them. They take food out of the refrigerator, take their portion, and leave the rest to spoil on the counter. Whatever they open stays that way until someone else comes in and completes the action. Very often, that person gets bonked in the head or knee by one of those open cabinet doors!

For the next 21 days, make the effort to finish whatever you start. I guarantee if you leave the kitchen cupboard doors open, you're leaving doors open all over the house. Don't believe me? Take a look at the doors and drawers in your bathroom or bedroom.

A famous Zen proverb proclaims, "The way a man does one thing is how he does everything." I think you'll discover that after you start completing simple, mindless actions such as closing cupboard doors and drawers, you will find yourself completing everything, from projects at work to promises to family and friends to the very thoughts you think. It isn't really about the cabinet doors and the dresser drawers; it's about the projects at work that take an act of Congress to finish or the unkept promises to family and friends. The cupboards and drawers are a metaphor for how you live your life.

Extra Ammo

Pantry moths often hide in packages of grain and flour and are difficult to eliminate. To prevent them from invading your kitchen, transfer your flours, cereals, and the like to airtight glass containers. My friend Chef Tanya Russell has the easiest solution of all. Put these products in the freezer for 10 to 15 minutes when you come home from the market. You'll kill any moths hatching in your products. In fact, if you have the freezer capacity, items such as grains, sugar, flour, and bread can live there until you need them.

Fresh Eyes Exercise:
The Kitchen

You want your kitchen to be a place you enjoy, whether you're cooking, eating, baking, planning meals, or just gazing out the window. Sit quietly in this room and pretend you have never been here before and know nothing about the occupants. What does the state of this room reveal to you? Start making your notes. You will probably notice two kinds of items: problem areas that need attention and creative ideas for the future.

For example, I noticed that my kitchen has a deep window that could fit a window box for growing herbs. I find the idea of being able to snip fresh herbs into tonight's dinner nurturing. What comes to mind for you? Take 8 minutes and write down your ideas. You'll be more focused and realistic after this exercise as you approach this wonderful (and, for many, daunting) room.

Speed Elimination: Papers

The usual culprits that make the kitchen feel overwhelming are the stacks of papers on the counters. How did I know, you ask? I see them in most homes. You walk in and drop the mail. The kids come home from school and add their homework and art projects. We get so busy we put off reading that newspaper, magazine, or favorite catalog. And so they multiply.

Now for 8 uninterrupted minutes, you're going to race around this room with a sturdy garbage or recycling bag in your hands and ditch those papers. (To protect against identity theft, shred any paper containing your social security number or account information.) Here are some things you may encounter that can leave home forever:

- Expired sales brochures and ads
- Catalogs (keep only the most current)

- Newspapers older than 1 day
- Magazines older than 1 to 2 months
- Newsletters older than 1 to 2 months
- Invitations to parties or events that have passed
- Credit card offers
- Bills that have been paid (unless they represent tax-deductible items)

Make sure you clear out the trash after this and any other organizing project. Doing so removes the possibility that you will change your mind and return items and enables you to experience how much lighter the room feels. And most importantly, this habit helps you learn to trust your judgment; constantly second-guessing yourself prevents you from moving forward in life.

Speed Elimination: Items That Don't Belong

A kitchen, especially if it's large, is often the burial ground for items we want to keep but need to deposit elsewhere in the home. Now is your chance. Did the dry cleaning get draped over a chair and forgotten? Are your child's art supplies piling up? Have over-the-counter medications and Band-Aids been languishing on the kitchen table? Make piles for different rooms in the home. After 5 minutes, distribute the items where they belong.

8 Minutes to a Nurturing Kitchen

The kitchen is full of items that are easy to toss and easy to organize. Let's get our organizing feet wet with a few simple actions that will produce big results.

Toss Old Kitchen Linens

Dish towels, pot holders, and aprons tend to multiply over time. Weed out your collection in 8 minutes and remember that small cotton items make great cleaning rags. Let the threadbare pot holders and the stained aprons go. The latter, however, might be repurposed as smocks during art projects if you have toddlers in the house who want to finger paint. If you store cloth napkins, tablecloths, and place mats in this room, give them the old once over as well. If you decide that an item has a use elsewhere, take it to the spot where you engage in that activity.

Fold and Stack

After you have whittled down your collection of pot holders, dish towels, and the like, spend a few minutes carefully folding and neatly stacking the ones you have decided to keep. You can even keep them in the same color order you have in your closet.

Eliminate Broken Equipment

Most people harbor the intention of fixing a piece of equipment that broke a long time ago. If you have been keeping a broken item for a year or more, toss it now or donate it to a charity that will repair it and sell it, such as Goodwill. Free up space for the things that do work.

If you're storing equipment in boxes, you're wasting space. Free that equipment, and you might find that you use it more often.

Clean as You Go

Most people pile dirty dishes, bowls, and cooking tools in the sink as they cook, creating unnecessary work. Why not clean as you go? Deposit dishes straight in the dishwasher rather than the sink. Rinse that bowl in seconds now rather than scrubbing caked-on food later. Clean the cutting board while you're waiting for a pot of water to boil. A quick wash here and another minute or two there, and you might just rescue a big block of time to read, watch the news, check your e-mail, or get to bed earlier.

Fluff and Fold

Do you have a few minutes while the next meal is simmering? Fold that laundry before the clothes get too wrinkled. Plus, you will no longer open the dryer to pop in wet clothes only to find your machine full from the previous day.

BUY IT: A STEP STOOL

To quickly and safely access the top shelves in your kitchen, purchase a two-step stool at your local home store. You can find inexpensive ones that fold up compactly and store easily between the refrigerator and the nearest cupboard. People frequently waste space with clutter, but it's equally wasteful to not use a cupboard or shelf because you can't reach it.

Create a Kiddie Korner

The universal toddler cry heard round the world is "let me do it!" Mastering tasks that mom, dad, and older siblings may have done for you is important to young children. Why not clear out an area in a low cabinet and put your children's plates, bowls, and cups at the proper height? These 8 minutes will help build their self-esteem.

After your children can access their own plates and bowls, they might like to fill them with food they select. Why not add some food designed for little hands and tiny bellies, such as small boxes of cereal and juice containers?

Organize Your Pet's Food

Your cat's or dog's dry food should be protected from critters and kept fresh. When you're at the home store picking up your organizing tools, why not get a container with a locking lid? I like the ones for dog food that are on wheels. You can slide the container under a cupboard in the kitchen or laundry room. Keep pet treats in a protected container, such as a simple glass jar or a decorative one if you have the counter space. If you have a cupboard dedicated to small cans of pet food, try a shelf creator to instantly double your space.

It won't take more than 8 minutes to pour the kibble into the new container, slide it under a cabinet or into a laundry room corner, transfer your pet's treats to an air-tight container, and arrange the canned food in a cupboard. Everyone in the family is now organized.

Pitcher This!

Are you always hauling out of drawers certain cooking utensils, such as your spatula or wooden spoons? Pop them into a pretty pitcher and keep them on the stove or a countertop. You'll save time by not having to open and close drawers every day. I bet you have a pitcher languishing in a cupboard that would be perfect for this task.

BUY IT: EVERYDAY DISHES & GLASSES

In many homes, the cupboard contains chipped everyday dishes and not enough drinking glasses. Stores such as Ikea carry inexpensive everyday dishes and glassware, so why not check your stash and see if it's time to go shopping.

After you toss the old ones and wash your new ones, take the time to arrange them in the cupboards. If you are pinched for space, use a shelf unit. I like the corner unit that separates dinner plates from salad plates, making it easy to pull out the size you need.

Stay Cool

Is a cooler taking up closet space? Stash it in the trunk of your car. You'll be able to pop perishable items in there so that they don't melt or spoil by the time you get home. If you don't have a cooler, pick up an inexpensive one the next time you go grocery shopping or wander into a home store.

Create an Instant Mudroom

Many families now commonly enter the home—and the kitchen—from the garage rather than the front door. Do you have an old, large serving tray? Set it next to the entry door to this room (or wherever you enter your home) and let it catch the water, snow, and mud from winter boots. If you don't have a large serving tray, pick up a boot tray.

8 Minutes to a Nurturing Kitchen

BASIC 8'S

The next section will really help you organize those pesky neglected kitchen areas. Expired spices, dull knives, and mystery items are about to be called to order.

Check Spices and Herbs for Freshness

My mother never understood why anyone would purchase the small size of any item if the large size were a better bargain. Dry spices and herbs, however, are good for six months to a year. Take the sniff test! Set your timer for 8 minutes, and sniff each spice and herb container in turn to check its freshness and potency. Note any you need to replace. Try shopping at your local natural foods store. The prices are usually much cheaper than your chain supermarket. If you need to buy a few spices in bulk, pick up some glass spice jars while you're at it. And here's an insider tip for finding spices in a flash: Store them in alphabetical order.

BUY IT: A SPICE RACK

You should store your spices in airtight containers in a cool, dry spot to preserve freshness. If spices are close to the stove, you are ruining the long-term potency of these delicate and expensive flavor enhancers. Many attractive spice storage options are available: a lazy Susan in a cabinet, an over-the-door unit, a drawer rack, or the ubiquitous wall-hung rack. Before shopping for a spice rack, assess your counter or cupboard space. If the storage unit is too big, it won't matter how beautiful it is.

Sharpen Your Knives

A common lament heard in kitchens is "I have to sharpen these knives." Indeed you do: A sharp knife is much safer than a dull one. Take out the knife sharpener and spend 8 minutes making your life easier. An electronic sharpener used every three months will keep your knives in tip-top shape for years of service.

Purge Mystery and Multiple Tools

In addition to mystery meat in the freezer, the average kitchen also has mystery tools—items you can't for the life of you identify. We're given these gizmos as gifts, we purchase them on a whim, or we get them as premiums at Tupperware or home-cooking parties. Our kitchens also hold space-eating collections of duplicate and triplicate items. How many garlic presses, potato peelers, or bottle openers do you have?

I can't see the number of drawers in your kitchen or what's inside, so you'll have to decide whether you can do this project in one 8-minute cycle or devote 8 minutes to each drawer.

As you open each drawer, make decisions quickly. For multiple items, save the best one. Then toss the duplicates in the trash or in a donation bag (but only if you will make the time to donate). Or if you can think of a legitimate place for one of these extra tools, such as a picnic hamper or cooler, put it there. For those mystery items, donate them or toss them, but do free up the space. I give my mystery items to Chef Tanya!

Separate Baking Tools

Keep cooking tools separate from baking tools. In addition, choose a drawer for cooking tools that's close to the pots, pans, and prep tools. Likewise, use a drawer for baking utensils that is close to baking pans, mixing bowls, and the like. When you need the garlic press, you don't want to have to shove cookie cutters and a rolling pin aside. If you want to truly organize like a pro, line the drawers and use drawer organizers.

Pare the Tupperware

I know some of you are saying, "Whew! I don't have to do this one because I don't have any Tupperware." But do you have disposable containers, such as the ones from the deli? (I call these "Tupperware light" because they serve the same purpose but don't last as long.) Or perhaps you've saved every glass jelly jar that ever entered your home?

These mismatched collections take up a huge amount of space and rarely get used. They fall into a category I call "fake prosperity"—any collection of items that are rarely utilized but that make you feel more affluent because you have so many. A bulging clothes closet, mountains of shoes, dated coats in the hall closet, toys that are no longer played with, stacks of magazines and catalogs—all give you a sense of fake prosperity.

BUY IT: A LID ORGANIZER

Consider yourself lucky if you have ample kitchen storage space to keep containers with their lids on. When you need one, you have the set. For other people, stacking containers by size and type works well, but the lids are always an issue. You can find an assortment of solutions in the kitchen section of your local home store. I like the unit that attaches to the back of a cabinet door and holds all types of lids, from container lids to those for your

pots and pans. Another solution, which you can find at The Container Store, is a pull-out lid organizer. It takes up little space and you can slide the unit toward you to retrieve the contents. If you have an average-sized collection and make speedy decisions, you won't need more than 8 minutes to pull out your stash of lids and return it pared and organized.

Most of my clients run screaming from the room at the mere mention of the word *Tupperware*. Take a deep breath and follow these few simple steps, and you will have a picture-perfect storage container cabinet:

1. Gather all of your containers in one place, such as the kitchen or dining room table. Be sure to put something down to protect the table's surface. Quickly divide the collection into type, such as square, round, glass, and take-out.
2. Match each bottom with a top.
3. Place the orphan pieces in the recycle bin or trash.
4. Review what remains. Often, people will retain a large collection of containers long after the family size has dwindled. If you don't use a container, toss or recycle it.

Unleash the Power of Prep

Shopping day usually finds us hurling purchases into the pantry, the cupboards, and the refrigerator as quickly as possible. Why not take 8 minutes to wash the fruits and vegetables you just bought before putting them away? The entire family can grab and go without you having to call out, "Did you wash that?"

Uncover the Front of the Refrigerator

Whenever I organize a client's kitchen, I know a potentially volatile conversation can erupt over the appearance of the refrigerator. Some (such as myself) prefer a pristine, bare front; others cloud every square inch with all manner of photos, notices, invitations, and personal notes. With that much stuff, the eye has no clue where to rest. Following are some choices you can make in minutes to improve the appearance of your refrigerator:

- **INVITATIONS:** Remove all invitations, checking the dates on each. Toss those for events that have passed. Enter the others in your calendar before tossing. If you need an address or directions from a flyer, keep it in your Pending file.
- **PHOTOS:** Remove the photographic mementos and either toss them or set them aside with the photos you are saving for a photo album or scrapbook. (Every family has a collection of photos stashed somewhere to be turned into an album on some future rainy afternoon. I touch on how to organize them when we get to the family room.)
- **HOLIDAY CARDS WITH PHOTOS:** After the holidays, feel free to toss these. The senders don't expect you to save the card forever; they hope you will enjoy seeing the progress their children have made over the past year. (If you are at odds with this solution, scan the photo into your computer, save the file in a central folder, and then toss the original photo.)
- **CONTACT INFORMATION:** Most parents have key phone numbers for family and medical practitioners along with local police and fire departments. Make sure any contact sheet is accurate and current. Remove outdated or multiple copies.
- **MAGNETS:** Pare your collection to no more than six. If you have a large collection, bag the overflow and rotate your magnets or use them elsewhere.

After you complete these steps, the entire kitchen will feel lighter and the information you do want to display will be easier to find.

8 Minutes to a Nurturing Kitchen

AMBITIOUS 8'S

You've come a long way, baby. Now you have an opportunity to really clear out those cupboards and counters. Any time spent bringing order to the most popular room in the home is time well spent. The entire family will benefit from these projects—maybe a few will pitch in and help you.

Wrap Grandma's China

This task requires three 8-minute rounds: inventory, transfer, and storage. I don't think I've ever been in a home that didn't have a set of good china for use on holidays. Traditionally, the set has been passed down from one generation to the next. These treasured pieces are often crowded into a kitchen cupboard where they take up much-needed space and are vulnerable to everyday accidents.

Round One
Inventory your china and buy a set of padded dish covers for them.

Round Two
Transfer the china. Start with the largest items and work your way down to the smallest. Work slowly and treat each

piece with care. Depending on the size of Grandma's bounty, you may need two sessions for this.

Round Three
Move your china to a better and safer space, such as one of the cupboards in the dining room hutch or a shelf you could empty or build in a dining room closet. Better still, use that cavernous cupboard on top of the refrigerator; it's a tough area to reach, which makes it ideal for a set of china you will probably use only once or twice a year.

Streamline Countertop Appliances
Moving things around on your counter is easy. Understanding where everything belongs before you start moving requires planning. Most people have had dysfunctional counters for so long that they no longer notice the incredible inconvenience.

Take a moment to look at your kitchen counters and consider the following:

- Do you take certain items out of a cupboard and use them every day? Could these items find a permanent home on the counter?
- Does the counter hold items that you rarely use, such as a mixer or food processor? Why not move these underutilized items to a cupboard or the pantry?
- Do you have an item you'd love to use every day, such as a juicer, but there's no room on the countertop and the device is too heavy to haul out each morning?
- Do you have just the right number of gadgets on the counter, but using them is inconvenient?

Spend just 8 minutes moving equipment into the areas where you use them. For example, create a breakfast zone on the counter for the coffeemaker and toaster or toaster oven. Place your mugs and coffee paraphernalia in the cabinet above the equipment, and you will save time and steps in the morning. Besides a breakfast area, how many other zones can you create?

Clean the Junk Drawer

Whenever I ask a client about their kitchen junk drawer, they are surprised that I know they have one. The secret is out: Everybody does! Take a deep breath and dive into this drawer. The following pointers should get you started. Set your timer and move fast:

- Everybody likes to have a hammer, a flathead screwdriver, and a Phillips head screwdriver handy. But if you have an entire tool chest in this drawer, transfer the excess to your literal tool chest.
- Keep a pen, pencil, highlighter, and Sharpie handy, and put the excess in a small plastic bag. Later, while you're watching TV or chatting with your best friend on the phone, check to see how many are viable.
- Retain one small pad of paper, and toss the million scraps of miscellaneous paper in the recycling bin.
- Review the mishmash of small items: pushpins, hair clips, paper clips, batteries, screws and nails, change, rubber bands, and buttons. Pare down whatever you have to a precious few and store the surplus where it belongs or get rid of it. An arts and crafts store, such as Michael's, carries plastic zip bags in assorted sizes.

Keep your "junk" in an appropriate size bag until you purchase a junk drawer organizer.

- Candy and gum leap into this drawer and stay until they are stale. Toss the old ones in the trash. Return the current stash to the drawer if this is where the family looks for such items. If you have lots of candy and gum, however, consider making space in the pantry and popping these items into a grid tote.
- Coupons love to live in this drawer. Toss expired ones. Trim the others, if necessary, and tuck them into an envelope. Next time you're in an office supply store, buy a durable envelope-style holder. Then you'll be able to toss your envelope in your purse or your car and not have it disintegrate over time.

A junk drawer rarely holds any sentimental items, so you shouldn't need more than 8 minutes to clear it.

BUY IT: A JUNK DRAWER ORGANIZER

If you are an ambitious sort and want your junk drawer to look picture perfect, pick up a single plastic drawer organizer that sports small and large compartments for all your assorted do-dads or several acrylic drawer organizers in various sizes. Another option is to place things on drawer liner and use small storage bags for the eclectic collection of tiny items.

Administer First Aid to the Pantry

I love a walk-in pantry. A space full of our favorite grub can be nurturing, but most times it's a thrown-together mess. You want to make your pantry as streamlined and functional as any supermarket.

Round One

Before you start to move pantry items around, do a speed-elimination. Are there items you no longer enjoy? It's better to toss something you will never use than to let it occupy valuable real estate. If you have a lot of items in this category, make a donation bag for your local shelter. Check expiration dates on all items.

Round Two

Next, take stock of what remains. You'll be keeping food items in categories, such as pasta, soup, and beans. If you have floor space, you could use it for heavy bottles of water and soda. Paper towels and napkins can live on the higher shelves. You want food at eye level. And you want the most popular items closest to the entrance so your family can do a quick grab and go. Plan to place less frequently used items behind the door.

Round Three

Depending on the size of your pantry, you might want to spend 8 minutes on each shelf. Then set your alarm and see how much you can accomplish in 8 minutes. You may be surprised!

Label Your Shelves

Now that you have a beautifully organized pantry, label each shelf to retain the order. Often we wonder why family members don't return items to their designated home;

they're probably unaware of what you have done. Let everyone know what you're doing and ask them to keep up the system. Tell them you are open to suggestions—you can always move a category and its label if you're offered a better idea!

BUY IT: KITCHEN STORAGE

You can organize a pantry (or the cupboards you're using as your pantry) without using any products. But I thought I would share my favorites in case you, like me, enjoy using tools that make your life easier:

- Remember the shelf divider I suggested for your closet? You can use a shelf divider here to demarcate the division of space on the shelf. Pasta and rice have one area, soup another, and so on. Dividers can make it easier to find things if you have a lot of people grabbing items.
- Grid totes help corral small items that can bleed across a shelf, such as packages of salad dressing, gravy, or instant drinks. Sort and toss into a grid tote.
- Are some of the shelves so high you have lost space? Pop in a portable shelf and divide the space in half. These shelves come in plastic or interesting materials such as bamboo. You can use them elsewhere, such as the linen closet.
- Put a series of cans on a shelf and what happens? All you can see are the ones in front. A shelf creator gives you three levels in one area. We used one on page 54 to sort pet food in a cupboard. These shelves come in three sizes: wide for bigger cans such as tomato sauce, medium for vegetable and bean cans, and narrow for small jars that hold spices or items such as

capers. Count your current stash of cans and see which sizes would best serve your needs. You can use shelf creators in the laundry room and inside bathroom cupboards.

- If you love baskets and have a large collection, you might use them in the pantry to store items such as potatoes.

You don't need to purchase any of these tools. Remember that a tool is useful only if it accommodates the items you have.

Make Over Your Refrigerator

Each week, many people toss spoiled food because it got lost in the mayhem on their refrigerator shelves. Does this happen to you?

You'd be amazed at the number of products designed to help organize the refrigerator. My favorite is the soda can dispenser that helps large families keep a dozen cans of beverages cold while not hogging much shelf space. But guess what? You don't need organizing products as much as you need to rearrange your food. If you devise a plan, it won't take more than 8 minutes to put into effect. For this project, I've divided your work into three sessions.

Round One

Assess the situation. Can you clearly see what's on each shelf? Is there any rhyme or reason where items are placed? Is the ketchup near mayonnaise and mustard or is it sitting in a sea of fruit? Next, take a deeper look and see if anything needs to be tossed. Take-home containers are probably number one on this list because they get shoved to the back of a shelf.

Round Two

Most modern refrigerators have designated areas for specific types of food. If you follow the guidelines, you won't have as much trouble as you might with an older model. Note the various categories of food. Most people have something along these lines:

Condiments
Dairy
Deli products
Drinks
Fruits
Meats
Vegetables

Round Three

Time to start moving and grouping your food!

Round Four

I'm sneaking in a possible fourth session should you have a large freezer compartment. It's great to separate food here, too, especially if you are freezing cuts of meat. Keep pork, chicken, and beef in separate zones. Make sure packages are clearly labeled and dated. Note also whether the contents were frozen raw or cooked. Mystery meat is the sad outcome of most meat wrapped and tossed into the freezer without a label.

Freezing does not mean forever. For guidelines on how long you should keep frozen meats, check out the guide on the U.S. Department of Agriculture website, at http://www.fsis.usda.gov/factsheets/focus_on_freezing/index.asp.

And do check the expiration dates on frozen packaged items such as vegetables, TV dinners, and desserts.

If you have lots of frozen dinners or other frozen meal packages, try standing them on their sides rather than laying them flat in a stack. Inevitably you'll want the one on the bottom, right? Plus, when the packages are on their sides, you can easily read the product name. We're going to use this trick again in the family room with another common household item (see page 129). You'll be surprised how much more efficient you can be turning items on their sides!

Confront the Madness under the Sink

In most homes, the area under the sink is a terrifying mess. The main tasks in this territory are eliminating and sorting.

Round One

Do you have young children or clever animals who can open cupboard doors? If so, your first task is to make sure the cupboard door has a lock. Cleaning products and bug sprays are poisonous; even if they aren't stored here now, you may store them here later.

We want to have easy access to the items; when the plumber comes one day, you don't want him to lose time hauling out numerous miscellaneous items. Let's take a look.

Round Two

Our next 8-minute round involves sorting and eliminating. First, clear out everything under the sink, grouping items into categories. You will no doubt find that you have several bottles or containers of one type of cleaner in use. Try to combine them and eliminate a few containers. While you're at it, check whether any of these products have expired, dried up, or in general look too funky to use. I bet you haven't seen some of these products in years.

Round Three

Your final 8-minute round consists of storing the items. If you want to use organizers, note the configuration of the pipes so you get a solution that fits. Here are some typical categories of under-the-sink items:

- **CLEANING TOOLS:** Sink scrub, dishwashing liquid, sponges, and the like are best kept handy in a heavy-duty rubber-type container that can handle the weight of all those liquids and powders. This type of container is also easy to clean. As mentioned, cleaning products are poisonous if ingested.
- **PLANT FOOD:** You might store plant food and vitamins under the sink. Sometimes there's even room for a small watering can.
- **BUG SPRAYS:** As noted, bug sprays are poisons. Never store human or animal food in the same area as a poison.
- **POLISHES:** Does your area hold silver or jewelry polish? I like to keep them separate from the other cleaners in a small container such as a grid tote.
- **GROCERY BAGS AND TRASH CAN LINERS:** I don't like to see folks store paper or plastic bags here because they usually float to the surface obscuring access to other

items. Save a few of each if you have a legitimate use for them and recycle the rest. In addition, create the habit of taking reusable bags to the store so you don't need to bring home paper and plastic bags. Under-the-sink is a good spot for trash can liners. But here's a tip: Before you put a fresh liner in the trash can, drop a few liners on the bottom of the can.

When you keep items in related groupings, you can quickly transform the under-sink area from a dumping ground to a vision out of a popular home design magazine.

A final note: If you shop at large home stores such as Costco, you probably have extra-extra-large sizes of cleaning products and the like. Transfer a portion of those large-size products to a small- or medium-size container, which you can then store under the sink for everyday or periodic use. Store the gigantic container in a separate location such as the garage or the laundry room. If you don't have a garage or laundry room, question the value of purchasing containers you have no place to store. The adage "Penny wise, pound foolish" comes to mind.

BUY IT: A SMALL FIRE EXTINGUISHER

Few homes have a fire extinguisher, and those that do generally have it in an inconvenient spot. Buy a small fire extinguisher and store it under the sink in a forward position that's easy to reach. If you have never used a fire extinguisher, I suggest that you purchase two and use one for practice. You want to be familiar with this lifesaving tool before you see flames!

Your New Kitchen Exit Ritual

Each time you leave the kitchen, take the following steps so that the space always feels welcoming:

- Put away all food.
- Put clean dishes in the cupboard.
- Place dirty dishes in the dishwasher.
- Wash any pots and pans. The exception is a pot or pan that needs to be soaked for a while.
- Return kitchen tools to their designated spot.
- Give the table and counter a quick wipe.
- Check the trash. If it isn't overflowing, it may be full of fresh food items such as banana peels, which will become aromatic over the next few hours. Consider a stainless steel or ceramic compost pail instead.
- If it's after dark, turn off the overhead light.

You may think that these tasks will take more than 8 minutes. I assure you, however, that from the starting point of a clean kitchen, completing these tasks will take only a few minutes.

For example, suppose you enter the (clean) kitchen for a snack on a Sunday afternoon. You make a sandwich and have a glass of milk. Before you sit down to eat, you return food items to the refrigerator. You have one dish, one glass, and perhaps some flatware to put in the dishwasher when you finish eating your lunch. You give the table and counter a quick wipe with a damp sponge. The garbage is fine and there's no light to switch off. Off you go.

What, as my dad asked me a million times in my childhood, was so hard about that? Give this the old college try for 21 consecutive days. Soon you will enjoy clear kitchen counters, a clean and empty sink, and cupboards that seem to hand you whatever tool you need. The room where everyone gathers will indeed be the most nurturing room in the home.

A Nurturing Kitchen

It stands to reason that the room we gravitate to will be more inviting if it's organized. We might be drawn to a beautiful kitchen, but if it harbors a chaotic collection behind cupboards and inside drawers, we won't enjoy the room as much because it's a struggle to find things. After a few 8-minute projects in the kitchen, you will have a more nurturing experience here as well as save time, money, and energy.

I'd like to end this section with a trick a client taught me years ago: buy a small lamp for the kitchen counter. In the evening, when all the dishes have been put away, turn on the lamp and turn off the overhead light. (If you don't have space for a lamp, use a dimmer switch.) Then when you visit the kitchen for a nighttime snack, you see the inviting soft glow of lamplight. Little touches like this make a house a home.

4 BATHROOM MINUTES

I am not discouraged, because every wrong attempt discarded is another step forward.

—THOMAS EDISON

No room is more vital—or falls into disarray more quickly and habitually—than the bathroom. The biggest culprits are a lack of systems and rituals. If your bathroom looks like a scene from a horror movie, I bet that each person exits the bathroom without looking back or thinking about the next user.

Your New Bathroom Exit Ritual

You may be wondering why I am presenting the bathroom ritual at the start of this chapter rather than at the end. In most rooms, the ritual will only be effective after some organizing has been done. But in the bathroom, the ritual can make a difference even if you never engage in a single 8-minute project. Imagine never again seeing a spray of toothpaste on your bathroom mirror or encountering a sticky residue on your counter. I bet you feel better already.

To ensure that the next user of the bathroom will find a clean, calm, well-organized environment, perform these steps as you prepare to exit the room:

- Wipe the counter.
- Clean the mirror.
- If the toilet seat needs to be wiped, swab the deck.
- Return your towel to the waiting towel bar or hook.
- Take any clothing you aren't going to wear with you as you exit. (Then hang up the item, toss it in the hamper, or add it to the dry cleaning bag.)
- If a nightgown, pair of PJs, or robe stays in this room, hang it on its hook.
- If you took out a product (such as hair gel or lipstick), return it.

Before you complain that these tasks take too much time to complete every time you leave the bathroom, breathe deeply! This list is comprehensive and probably reflects your last visit in the morning before you leave for work. Do these tasks on an as-needed basis and they usually won't take more than 90 seconds tops. Here's a tip: For fast cleanups, keep a colorful sponge on the counter or use a disinfectant wipe in a pop-up dispenser.

Life Tweak

What is more demoralizing than a bathroom counter coated with layers of hair gel, hairspray, toothpaste, make-up, shaving cream, and whatever else your family uses? This chapter's life tweak is simple: All family members should cultivate the habit of checking the counter as they exit. If the counter needs to be wiped, do it.

Extra Ammo

Because cosmetics tend to be so expensive, we like to keep them forever. Unfortunately, the shelf life of the average cosmetic is far from forever. In this section, I provide some expiration guidelines, but before you read them, you need to know how to "break the code." FDA law mandates that all manufactured makeup have a batch code or lot code on or under the label or in the tube crimp that records when the makeup was produced. The code is usually three to five digits or letters, and unfortunately brands and labs use different systems. You can, however, relay the code to customer service to discover the age of the makeup. For example: F61 in Jouer language stands for June 2006, first batch that month.

The following guidelines are from my client Sarah Garcia, the (former) director of Product Development at Jouer Cosmetics. (These tips have also appeared in *One Year to an Organized Life.*)

- **ANYTHING WITH SPF:** Examples include powders, gloss, lipstick, and foundation. Toss after two years! Most SPF chemicals are good for two to three years in cosmetics. You don't want to use anything that has expired.

- **POWDERS:** These products, such as eye shadow or blush, last much longer than you might think. Most are good for up to five years, but pigments can change over time and oils used in powder can dry out, making them chalky and dry. Test the product on your skin. If it applies nicely, keep it; otherwise, toss it.

- **WAX-BASED PRODUCTS:** These products, such as lipstick and cream blushes, tend to have a long shelf life, often three to five years. Follow the same advice as with powders: Test it before using.

- **WET LIP-GLOSS AND LIQUID FOUNDATIONS:** These items should be tossed after one to two years because the ingredients often start to separate.

- **MASCARA:** If your mascara has been opened and is older than six months—toss it. Sealed, mascara can last a few years.

These guidelines will take the guesswork out of the elimination process later in the chapter, when you work on organizing your cosmetics.

Fresh Eyes Exercise: The Bathroom

Enter the bathroom with a clear mind, a notebook, and a pen. Give yourself 8 minutes to look at this room with fresh eyes. What do you notice? You might see towels and clothing over the floor and be instantly annoyed that your family members simply don't pick up after themselves. But does the room have enough towel bars, hooks, and shelves? Often the big issue with the bathroom is that it needs a little help to function at its best. Ask yourself the following questions:

- Does the bathroom have any hooks? If so, could it use more? Do you need beautiful brass hooks or would plastic ones with adhesive backing do?
- Would adding a few shelves help relieve the congestion on the counter?
- Would an over-the-toilet unit be useful? Some are just shelves but others also have a closed cupboard for items you'd like to keep private.
- Could some towels be stored under the sink?
- Would the shower area benefit from a shower caddy?

Set your timer. List your issues. Figure out some possible solutions. Start a shopping list. If you're stumped, I hope the material in this chapter inspires you.

Speed Elimination: The Bathroom

Set your timer for 8 minutes and toss without thinking. Put items in a trash bag or a recycling box. You do more thoughtful eliminations later. One caveat: If you share this room with someone else, do not toss anything that does not belong to you. Ready. Get Set. Eliminate!

If you want to tackle the entire bathroom yourself, be sure to get permission to touch the belongings of others. Many people appreciate having someone else sort and organize for them, but no one likes to have their stuff tossed. Perhaps you can set aside a pile of candidates for review?

8 Minutes to a Spa Experience

QUICKIES

Take a deep breath and get ready to dive into the world of the bathroom. Perhaps no other room in the home (except the pantry) holds so many mistakes: the prescription you never finished, the lipstick that looked dark red in the store and hot pink on your lips, and, oh yes, the hair mousse that gave you helmet head. Time to give them the heave-ho and reclaim valuable real estate.

Toss Old Prescriptions

Cleaning out the medicine cabinet doesn't take long but can be overwhelming. I have a theory why: The cabinet is usually full of expired but expensive prescription drugs and you don't want to let them go. But medications will only get older and less efficacious sitting there.

Devote a few minutes to eliminating expired prescription medications. (You deal with the cabinet's other items later.) Do not flush medicine down the toilet or pour it down the drain. Doing so can pollute your city's water supply. Ask your pharmacy to dispose of them.

Consolidate Cold Care

It makes sense to have a stash of cold and cough remedies so that you can find relief should a bug strike suddenly. Spend 8 minutes and gather all products in this category. Check expiration dates. Make a list of any items you are running low on or need to replace. If you have opened several bottles of something such as aspirin, see if you can consolidate into one container. Depending on where you store your cough and cold medicines, you could store them in a grid tote from The Container Store or simply recycle a shoebox.

Consider Your Hamper and Trash Basket

Very often the hamper and trash basket in the bathroom are small to conserve space. But if these two receptacles are always overflowing, you need to rethink your choices. Consider how you will solve these issues.

- Do you need to purchase a new hamper or trash can? Where will you place it? Take measurements to be sure the one you choose will fit perfectly.
- Can you use the current hamper or trash can elsewhere, such as in a child's room?
- Might a hamper or trash can from another room work here?

Clean Out Old Towels

The next 8-minute adventure is to examine your towels. I mean your entire towel collection, not just the ones hanging in the bathroom this minute. Are any threadbare, stained, faded, or full of holes? Is it time to put towels on your shopping list?

Some people recycle towels as rags. That's a wonderful idea, unless you end up with a veritable rag explosion. Set aside one or two for your pet, for bathing or wiping muddy paws. In addition, your local vet or emergency animal hospital always needs old sheets, towels, and blankets. You won't get a tax deduction but you will be doing something wonderful for an animal in need.

Let's talk turkey, or should I say hemorrhoids? Doctors say extended periods of time sitting on the toilet can lead to hemorrhoids. If you can't live without magazines and newspapers, however, at least clean out your stash so that every choice is current. And of course keep them contained so that they aren't splayed out over the floor.

8 Minutes to a Spa Experience

BASIC 8'S

You've faced down the medicine cabinet monster and those pesky expired prescriptions. Let's get brave and sort through everyday and first aid remedies. These products really eat up cabinet space in most homes, especially those with young children. After you tame these categories, every other project in this section will seem like a breeze.

Organize First Aid Items
As with cold remedies, every home has an array of general remedies. These vary depending on the family's common

ailments. Preparation H, sunburn cream, itch remedies, Tums, and earwax removal are but a sampling.

Once again, gather your stash, check expiration dates, and toss. Add to your shopping list whatever needs to be replaced or fortified. I suggest using a large grid tote to store this category of items.

Large families tend to have lots of general care items, more than can fit in even a large grid tote. For this situation, divide products into subcategories and put them in their own container. For example, sunblock and sunburn remedies can easily fill a small grid tote. Remove the tote from the bathroom during the off-season. Or if you slap on sunblock before you leave the house, keep this container in the hall closet or the mudroom.

Bandages, gauze, and small braces for things such as sprained ankles can fill their own container. There's no sense wading through sunscreen when all you need is a Band-Aid!

Another way to tame an unruly category is to create a main container that stays in the bathroom and have backup supplies in another location, such as a nearby linen closet. However, you'll have to train yourself to check the satellite container when you're running low on a product rather than simply buying more.

BUY IT: A PORTABLE SHELF

If your linen closet isn't large but you have at least one deep shelf, you can pop in a portable shelf from the home store. Then you could store several smaller containers instead of one large one.

Rethink Your Paper Product Storage

A good time to think about where you store paper products is when you come home from a shopping trip. Most people buy their paper products in large quantities. But if you shop at a big box store such as Costco, it's almost impossible to store all your tissues and toilet paper in one bathroom. What's a consumer to do?

First ask yourself how often you need a new box of tissues and a fresh roll of toilet paper. Your answer will determine how much to keep in reserve in the bathroom. Following are some typical areas for storing paper products:

- An over-the-toilet unit
- An open shelf
- A deep drawer
- Under the sink
- A free-standing toilet paper holder

After you store some supplies in your bathroom within easy reach, you will still have several boxes of tissues and rolls of toilet paper in need of a home. The four areas that usually come to the rescue are the linen closet, under the guest bathroom sink, the laundry room, and the garage. If you can set up a baker's rack outside the door that leads into the house from the garage, you can store lots of overflow from your pantry here as well. By the way, if you have multiple bathrooms, distribute supplies to all so that no one is caught shorthanded.

Assign a Bathroom Monitor

Children need chores, so assign one to be the tissue and toilet paper monitor. Ask your child to check on the bathrooms once a week and replenish the stock as needed. If you create a shopping list, your child can add items to it as needed. The bathroom abounds with chore assignments. A child can check the hamper and take dirty towels to the laundry room, wipe off the counter, empty the trash when full and replace the trash bag or liner, and squeegee the shower stall. Rotate such chores so that every child gets a turn. Remember to assign age-appropriate chores.

Create Satellite Stations

A satellite station doesn't refer to a place for Scotty to beam you up. After you've sorted through your first aid, general supplies, makeup, hair care, and body lotion collections, ask yourself if it would behoove you to have some extra kits made up either for other parts of the home or elsewhere. For example, you may want a minicollection of common staples such as Band-Aids, medicated first aid ointment, and a thermometer in the kitchen to take care of common scrapes and burns. Or you might want an overnight makeup kit handy, or perhaps a combo first aid/overnight kit in the trunk of your car? These kits are easy and fun to create. They can also give new life to excess products you were considering tossing or passing on to others. Most of my clients have too many makeup bags. This is a wonderful way to recycle them.

8 Minutes to a Spa Experience

AMBITIOUS 8'S

These next projects take a bit more time but are guaranteed to deliver that spa experience we all crave. You will never see a cluttered spa. They all provide a clean Zen-like atmosphere that invites us to relax and forget our cares for awhile. Why not enjoy that experience at home?

Untangle Hair Products

Commercials for hair care products abound. If you want the perfect partner, a great career, and a bulging bank account, you have to purchase the right styling gel. So skilled are these ads that they make products we don't need irresistible. I think this is why most bathrooms I organize contain mountains of shampoo, conditioner, gels, mousses, and pomades. Before you begin this project, take a minute to survey your bathroom. Are all hair-related products in one location? If not, follow these steps to help you get this product line under control.

Note that those with minimal hair products can do all of these steps in 8 minutes. But if you have long, beautiful tresses or live with a bevy of teenage girls, take heart. You can turn each step into an 8-minute project and take a few days to complete them all. You'll earn no demerits on the road to success.

Round One

Gather all shampoos and conditioners in one spot. Toss any that have separated, hardened, or have lost favor with you. If you don't use it, lose it. If you tried a product once or twice but know you won't use it again, don't let it rob you of valuable space. If you really can't bear to throw something out, set it aside for your guest bathroom, if you have one. (When your cousin Gwen exclaims how much she enjoyed the shampoo, you can be magnanimous and give it to her. It will be our secret.) Or make a care package for an equally hair-obsessed friend. Finally, if you have multiple bottles of any product, consolidate and toss the empties.

Round Two

Return to the shower only the shampoos and conditioners you intend to use. Rather than turn the shower into a mini Costco, store your backup supplies elsewhere—under the sink, in the linen closet, inside a bathroom cupboard, or down the hall in the guest bathroom. If you have more than two or three extra bottles, consider using a grid tote so the bottles don't get separated. ("I was sure I had another bottle of shampoo in here somewhere.") If you purchased a multipack of bottles, remove the excess packaging.

BUY IT: A SHOWER CADDY

If you are in the market for a simple container for your shower products, I suggest buying a shower caddy. One with a handle makes life easier when you need to move all those products on cleaning day. If you prefer the kind that hang, with your cell phone snap a picture of the configuration of your bathtub or shower area so you won't forget any details when you go to the store.

Round Three

Now it's time to sort your hair care products. Follow the same guidelines we used in round one. Make separate piles for mousses, gels, pomades, and any other styling products you use. The easiest way to keep these products together is to store them in a grid tote. Put one of each item in this tote, and then store the tote in a deep drawer or under the sink. In the morning, only one move is required to take out everything you need and another move to put it back in place.

If you have an extensive array of backup products, you probably never knew what was on hand so you made unnecessary purchases or you shop exclusively at big box stores. If possible, store backup products under the sink. Otherwise, buy a large grid tote and put your backup stash in a nearby cupboard in the linen closet or guest bathroom. If you're lucky, your shampoo and conditioners will fit in one container.

Remember too that lotions, potions, shampoos, conditioners, and gels, just like cosmetics, don't last forever. Many have expiration dates. If the supersize starts to separate before you get to it, you've wasted money and space. A bargain isn't always a bargain, so be sure you're getting one.

Round Four

If you have a large collection of hair dryers, curling irons, and brushes, keep it contained in one area, preferably near your styling products. If you use some of these tools only on special occasions and space is limited, store these tools elsewhere. Your bathroom drawers and cupboards should be like the command station of the *Starship Enterprise*. Captain Kirk didn't have a lot of extraneous tools hanging around, did he? Neither should you. Every miscellaneous item is going to slow you down and eat critical minutes you need to get out of the house on time. Although I generally advocate keeping every item in a category with its brethren, I often bend that rule in the bathroom to accommodate the space available, the amount of products and tools in question, and the number of people using the room.

Eliminate Old Makeup

Ladies, take a deep breath. I know that throwing away makeup is a sensitive issue. We spend a small fortune on cosmetics each year. We have our favorites and love to experiment. But if we aren't judicious, we wind up with a lot of rapidly expiring, caking, drying, outdated makeup.

Read the "Extra Ammo" section on page 77 again carefully. Then gather all makeup products and move quickly while following these simple steps to success:

- Fearlessly dive in and toss the items that have expired.
- Make a pile of items you used once and know you won't ever touch again, and toss these. (Or offer them to your best friend or teenage daughter if you don't want to toss them.)
- When your stash is whittled to what you actually use, see if you can divide the pile into everyday products versus special occasion makeup. Glitter and purple mascara don't work at the grocery store or the office.

Most women have lots of makeup bags. Place your special occasion and evening products in one of them. Depending on the available space, you might keep this bag in the back of a bathroom drawer, the back of the undersink area, or on a closet shelf. The ultimate placement depends on how often you will grab this makeup bag: once a year indicates the closet might be ideal, while every weekend means keep it close at hand.

- The ideal way to display your everyday makeup is in a shallow top drawer. I use a drawer liner so items don't roll around and clear drawer organizers, which are easy to clean and come in a variety of shapes. Sort your products so that eye makeup, lipstick, gloss, blush, and tinted moisturizer aren't lumped in a heap. Place in the medicine cabinet any items too big for a drawer.
- When you get to the end of this 8-minute session, see if some makeup bags can be tossed, passed on to teenage daughters, or given to charity.

BUY IT: A MAKEUP ORGANIZER

A few of my clients must have a variety of makeup tools and products available at all times. They keep everything in a large, professional makeup case and place it on the counter each morning. Teenage girls often need the same setup but in a smaller case. Another solution you might employ is to use a variety of makeup bags to store your product categories and then keep all the individual containers in a grid tote that you pop out each morning as you prepare for your day. Or you might want to store makeup on the counter in acrylic containers.

The solution needs to suit your age, profession, and love of cosmetics. No one size fits all when it comes to solving the riddle of organizing makeup.

Contain Everyday Supplies

I find all manner of things stashed under the bathroom sink. Remember that pipes spring leaks, and you don't want to have to haul out a million loose, drenched products in an emergency. With a few containers, you can empty this area in seconds. Depending on what you need to keep under the sink, you might use a combination of grid totes, a portable shelf, or plastic drawers. I keep first aid, general health care, and backup supplies in three stackable drawers on the left side of the area under my bathroom sink. Everything is accessible, dry, and clean. On the right side, I have small grid totes for items I use frequently. Extra toilet paper and tissues are in the undersink area of my guest bathroom.

Round One

Spend these 8 minutes on an archaeological dig under your sink. Don't pull everything out for this go-round. Just take a look and see what you have and toss what you can. If you see items you realize could be stored outside this room, remove them and, when the buzzer sounds, take them to their new home.

Round Two

Think about what you have stored under the sink and which products would work best for containing and organizing it all. After you gather the tools you need, dedicate another 8 minutes to this area. Now you can indeed take everything out (keeping items grouped around you in categories) and then return it in an organized fashion. Don't be surprised if you toss more things.

When an area is particularly difficult or emotional, break it into phases. This will allow you to make steady progress without being overwhelmed. You don't want your fear of success or failure to cause you to throw in the towel. We want to fold that towel and put it in its place!

A Spa-like Bathroom

Other than a staff of people who can take care of your every need, one aspect of a spa is how wonderful it smells. Unless you dislike fragrance, it can be nice to introduce scented candles or an oil diffuser to the bathroom. If you want to investigate the world of aromatherapy, choose a fragrance to lift your spirits (citrus), help you get to sleep (lavender), quiet the mind (sandalwood), or feel sexy (peppermint).

The second key ingredient when it comes to the creation of a spa-like experience is a Zen organized environment. You've done the hard work; now it's time to relax and enjoy your rewards. Do you have treats such as a tray for the bathtub and a pillow so you can soak and read at the same time? This is the perfect room for a dimmer switch in case you'd rather soak and listen to your favorite songs on your iPod. Life can be a struggle; an organized, well-maintained bathroom offers an antidote to the stresses and strains of life.

5 PAPER CLUTTER MINUTES

Simplicity is the ultimate sophistication.

—LEONARDO DA VINCI

Every day we get bills, newsletters, brochures, catalogs, postcards, business information, invitations, school communications, and children's artwork—the list is endless. What to do with it all, especially now that the kitchen is organized and you'd like to keep those counters clear? The heart and soul of your office—and by office, I mean any designated space where you carry on the business of your life—needs a functioning file system, an easy-to-locate repository for the active papers in your life. Want to know whether you paid a bill or filed a medical claim or responded to Joe and Erin's wedding invitation? When you have a system, you will be able to find the answer in less than a minute.

Your first quickie project is the creation of what I call action files. From those files, you can learn the basics of a file system. From this moment on, you can rejoice because all incoming papers will have a home. All you will need to do is ask questions about their ultimate importance in your life. Whether they land in the trash, the recycler, or a folder, at least they won't be piled up on your kitchen counters, your desk, or the floor!

Most people keep too much paperwork because they are afraid they will make a mistake and toss something important. In truth, simple guidelines can help you. Not sure if a receipt is a tax deduction or how long to keep papers related to investments? Ask your tax person. What about papers related to real estate? Ask your real estate agent or real estate attorney. For every question, someone in your life has the latest information. Saving everything "just in case" is not the right approach. When you clear out your workspace of unnecessary paper, you will enhance your ability to think more clearly and will do your best work in your home office.

Your New Paper Ritual

The way paper is dealt with needs to be ritualized so a free-for-all doesn't ensue when the mail comes into the home. As a bonus, your children can learn from you how to handle mail, pay bills in a timely fashion, and set up a file system—a valuable set of life skills. If children see you constantly fretting about the mail and finances, they too will learn those responses. The unconscious message is: "Paper is scary and hard to manage." If your child has trouble keeping track of homework assignments and completing projects, ask yourself if he or she is following the model that exists elsewhere in the home. A few simple steps can make it all easier!

1. Deposit the mail and all other important papers entering the home in a designated container.
2. Deal with the newly deposited material at the same time every day.
3. Sort the mail, eliminating as much as you can from the stack.
4. Place all items that need your attention or retention in the appropriate action file.
5. Schedule items on your calendar if necessary.

BUY IT: A BASKET FOR THE MAIL

You'll want to have a container ready to catch your mail and other papers. Baskets designed to hold newspapers are the ideal size, with a large, flat bottom to protect items that shouldn't be bent (such as your child's artwork or important legal documents). The one I use is from The Container Store, measures 17-7/8" × 13-3/4" × 5-1/8" high, and is made of lucky bamboo. If you want, toss in a letter opener so you always have one handy.

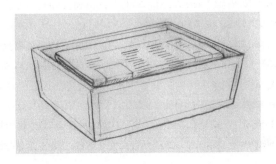

Step 1: Deposit the Mail

When you walk in the door with the mail, you probably follow a ritual, albeit an unconscious one. Despite that ritual, the mail probably gets scattered, lost, or simply swallowed up in an existing pile. The addition of one basket for depositing paper changes the landscape. We learn through repetition, so if it takes a week or so for you to get in the habit of depositing your mail in the basket, be patient. Stop and start as many times as you need until you get your 21 consecutive days under your belt. After that, you won't have to think about this task because the habit will be established.

Step 2: Set a Time to Deal with the Mail

Ritualize when you will sort through each day's stack of mail. Some people like to sort their mail as soon as they walk in the door. Others like to wait for a quiet time in the evening. The time you choose isn't important as long as you hold the designated time sacred. In other words, make sorting the mail a habit.

Step 3: Sort and Toss

The first thing you must do is whittle the pile down. After you get the hang of sorting and tossing, you will become not only speedy but ruthless. You'll see that 8 minutes is way too generous for this task. But allow that skill to develop over time and be content to start a little slowly and hesitantly. Flip through the pile looking for junk mail, which is a no-brainer category to eliminate right off the top. (I shred anything with my name and address on it and recycle the rest.)

Next, divide your mail into broad categories, such as bills, business, and personal. Place catalogs, magazines, and advertisements that interest you into a separate pile to be dealt with last. Open all of the mail and toss or recycle the extraneous matter such as the envelope the material arrived in and any advertisements. As you eliminate the excess paper, the shrinking pile will give you a sense of control.

Step 4: File Your Mail

Now that you've sorted your mail, it's time to file it in the appropriate action files. Grab a few manila folders (or go crazy and buy colored folders or fancy files if you feel that color or style will more easily draw you to this task). Then label them with the action items that suit your needs. A label maker creates clear, easy-to-read labels, but you can handwrite them too.

Here are the most common action files:

- Pending
- To Call
- To Do
- To File
- To Pay
- To Read

You might want to refine this list to suit your needs. For example, some people separate To Do items into those items that need some kind of action from those that need only a phone call to handle. If that type of organization is requested, I create the following:

- Bills
- Pending
- To Call
- To Do
- To File
- To Read

I do not have separate To Do and To Call folders, but I divide my To Do folders into To Do: High Priority and To Do: Low Priority based on time pressure, priority, or level of importance, as follows:

- Bills
- Pending
- To Do: High Priority
- To Do: Low Priority
- To File
- To Read

The humble file folder is the key to your success. Place your action files in the front of your file cabinet, in the file drawer in your desk, or in an inexpensive portable file caddy. Later, when you are ready to do the action required, all the material will be waiting for your attention.

By the way, I often see clients who toss papers directly into a hanging folder. This system is highly inefficient— every time you need to retrieve a paper, the stack needs to be resorted. Instead, place similar items into a file folder and then put that folder into a hanging file folder. I keep all my action files in alphabetical order in one 2-inch-wide box-bottom hanging file folder.

Step 5: Schedule Action Items on Your Calendar

As you can see, this system will absorb your mail and transform it from a pile into actionable segments. Take care of as many of the new details as you can immediately to make your scheduled work sessions less daunting. (The mail usually brings new tasks, doesn't it?)

If the baby has colic, your spouse has the flu, or you are so weary you can't see straight, just pop the material into your action folders. The ideal, however, is to schedule a specific time to deal with your action folders each day. You can be flexible for family emergencies, but if an emergency occurs every day at the time you have set aside to work, you need to deal with the underlying fear. Establishing this habit helps you gain control over your mail and ultimately the business aspect of your life.

When you look at a personal calendar, you see a snapshot of your life. Without one, you are subject to whims, delays, and every avoidance tactic in the book. However, you need to decide what kind of calendar speaks to you. Whether it's paper or electronic, it's your new best friend. Keeping a calendar is important—so important, in fact, that I made it this chapter's Life Tweak.

Life Tweak

Again, one of the most powerful tools in your organizing arsenal is a calendar, but its power depends on your devoted usage. Every morning, check your calendar to see what you need to accomplish that day. Then check it again before you retire or while you are sorting the mail. I like the month-at-a-glance layout so I can also judge the demands on my time. Am I overscheduling or am I giving myself an unearned holiday? Are work assignments balanced with times of rest?

After you sort your mail, have your calendar with you so you can note upcoming key days and appointments in your life. This way, nothing important slips through the cracks. Go to your local office supply store and check out the calendar selections if you aren't already devoted to a particular system. Ask friends and colleagues what works for them, but ask the organized ones! And don't overlook the calendar on your smartphone, in Outlook, or in Google Calendar. Each has wonderful features and advantages. Make your decision based on the number of people in your life and the complexity of your schedule.

Extra Ammo

You want to stay on top of your bill paying because making regular, on-time payments is an essential factor in a good FICO credit score. If you have an upcoming big-ticket transaction, such as buying a home, refinancing your mortgage, or leasing a car, your FICO score will determine not only whether you can complete the transaction but also how much interest you will pay.

Fresh Eyes Exercise: The Home Office

When it comes to a home office, the most common complaint I hear is something along these lines: "I don't know why, but I don't enjoy working in my office. I have a desk and a file cabinet, but I never come in here." When I enter the room, I instantly know the issue thwarting my client's efforts to pay bills and deal with paperwork: The room is confused. It usually has a dual focus, such as home office and guest room, gym, or craft room. Is that the case in your home office? Or is your office even smaller, such as a kitchen nook or a portable file box in your living room? You need to take stock of the setup no matter how creative, chaotic, or crowded your situation is.

Take 8 minutes to sit in and quietly observe this room. What do you notice? If your office also serves as a guest room, is the bed overwhelming the room? Is the closet so packed that you have no place to store office supplies? Does the room need a bookcase, or does the existing one need to be cleared? Is the bookcase too large or too small? If you share your office with your hobbies, are craft supplies on every available surface?

Often a combo room is thrown together with little thought or planning. As you notice all the now-obvious reasons why you don't use or don't enjoy using this room, start crafting a plan to change it.

Sometimes the fresh eyes exercise reveals a change in the family dynamic. For example, that huge bed is no longer needed because your parents are now in assisted living and no longer visit. You may be better served by a futon that opens up for the occasional overnight guest and serves you as a couch. If you leave the futon opened up as a bed, your bill-paying area will quickly become your nap-time zone.

Is the room set up in a way that promotes your ability to think clearly? Is the lighting adequate? Is the desk too big or not large enough? Do you have too many plants, or could the room benefit from some? Make a few notes and see what you need to do to make this room support you.

Speed Elimination: The Home Office

Now that you have looked at your home office with new eyes and listed what needs to be changed, it is time for a speed elimination. This exercise is a carbon copy of the one we did in the kitchen because most people have paper debris on the counters. The goal is to divest this room of extraneous paper so you can think clearly and do your best work. You don't want to avoid using the room for the next 6 months while you slowly make the physical transformation needed. With this 8-minute investment of time, you will clear a workspace.

Tear through the space looking for the following items:

- Expired sales brochures and ads
- Catalogs older than 1 month
- Newspapers older than 1 day
- Magazines older than 1 to 2 months
- Newsletters older than 1 month
- Invitations to events that have passed

For most of these items, trust that any information you need will find its way to you or be available to reference on the Internet.

Take a deep breath and remind yourself that success involves completing one step at a time. When you finish, you will have your action files, a clear space on which to work, and, if necessary, a plan to transform a room in your home into a functioning office. The files are key to your success. You can still do great work if the only surface you have is the dining room table for 20 minutes a day or an office nook in the kitchen.

8 Minutes to Paper Peace

QUICKIES

Paper frightens most of my clients. The quickies in this chapter will give you a handle on your paper world, especially now that you've cleared out a bit of the debris and taken stock.

Use Direct Deposit

Do you work for one employer and have a set salary? Save yourself weekly trips to the bank by setting up direct deposit for your paycheck. The process shouldn't take more than one phone call to your payroll department and an appointment with them to fill out the necessary forms—be sure to bring your social security number and a voided check so they have your account and routing numbers. If your company allows you to receive your pay stub online, sign up for this option; be sure to create an online folder for storing your online pay stubs.

Create a Pending Folder

I tell my clients to check their To Do folders daily. But what happens when you take care of something and have to wait for a response, such as a medical reimbursement? Instead of looking at that paper every day, put it in the Pending folder and check that folder once a week to see whether you need to take additional action. Did you add a Pending folder to your action files? Take a minute to do so now.

Stay Healthy!

Now is the perfect time to note on your calendar a reminder to make appointments for annual physical and tests (such as a mammogram), immunizations for school or travel, and dentist visits for everyone in the family. By the way, have Fifi and Fido been to the vet lately? To avoid overwhelming yourself with hours of calls, make a few each day.

Don't Dread the Shred

Many of my clients have a paper shredder but also have all manner of mental blocks about it. They either shred everything (a time-consuming process) or shred nearly nothing but accumulate material to be shredded until it's a daunting mound of paper. Why not take today's mail and practice for a few minutes? In general, you want to shred documents with your name, address, and social security number; account numbers; or your mother's maiden name. Don't shred every page of a credit card offer; shred just the application form imprinted with your name and address. Shred envelopes addressed to you but recycle the return address envelopes. You get the idea. Remember that some shredders can't handle paper clips and staples. (If you buy a shredder, be sure to get a cross-cut shredder because paper cut in strips can be reconstructed. A good shredder is your first line of defense in the war on identity theft.)

Connect the Family

Get a huge calendar and hang it behind the door of the kitchen or family room. Put all family member appointments here so that you don't double-book someone. In the event of an emergency, you will also know where everyone is currently located. If your children are older and every family member is addicted to a smartphone, use a community calendar such as Google. You can even keep local aunts, uncles, close family friends, and grandparents in the loop.

8 Minutes to Paper Peace

BASIC 8'S

Pockets of chaos abound when it comes to paper. Let's continue to rout them out, including those pesky cash receipts, your beloved briefcase, and those ubiquitous tax receipts from years past that clog every home.

Simplify Your Banking

If you own a computer, it behooves you to learn how to access both your checking and your credit card accounts electronically. After you set up your online access and get comfortable with the process, you can make payments and check your balance in no time. Have your statement and bills sent by e-mail and save a tree—as well as reduce paper clutter. I bet you never realized how many options you had to save trees and clutter.

Find a New Home for Income Tax Receipts

Do you have a four-drawer file cabinet but it is full of tax backup material? Uncle Sam does require that you save certain receipts for an extended period, but the best place to store this material is in boxes you can shove to the back of your office supply closet. Your file cabinet is meant to make current information available to you at a moment's notice.

First separate the actual tax returns from the backup material.(As time goes by, you will be able to shred or re-cycle the backup material. Uncle Sam doesn't require you to keep them forever.) If possible, store the returns them-selves in a fireproof metal box. Put the backup material in a cardboard box, label the box clearly, and then find a spot suitable for long-term storage. If you are a homeowner, you might place a four-drawer metal file cabinet in your garage just for tax material and anything else you might want to archive (such as home remodel records and work projects). Be sure the cabinet locks and designate a spot for the key.

Streamline Your Briefcase

I don't want you to stop using your briefcase, laptop bag, or tote bag for work, but I do want you to spend 8 minutes cleaning it out. Try to boycott the use of your briefcase or bag as a lunch box, trash can, file cabinet, or Staples outlet. When I clean out briefcases for my clients, I typically end up with a pile of items that belong elsewhere, such as the following:

- Stale gum, candy bars, health food bars, tea bags, and fast food items such as ketchup or sugar
- Papers from projects long completed or abandoned
- More office supplies than a room full of executives could use in an afternoon
- Convention premiums that will never be used

Make it a habit to clean out your briefcase regularly. You never know when one of those mustard packets will decorate one of your important papers! Avoid the risk.

Check Your Office Supplies

You don't want to be in the middle of a project and discover that you need a paper clip or highlighter. Are your backup supplies handy? Take a minute to see whether you need to add such critical items as copy paper, fax paper, and printer cartridges to your shopping list.

Likewise, when you overbuy supplies, you waste space and money. Gather what you know you will never use and find a friend, colleague, or family member who will use them—donate or toss the rest. Remember, Sharpies, highlighters, and pens dry up eventually, and your stash may be defunct when you are finally ready to use it. The next time you're moved to take advantage of a sale, ask yourself if you are being penny wise but pound foolish.

Unsubscribe Your Way to Freedom

When you're at the computer, why not reexamine your need to receive the glut of newsletters, catalogs, and sale updates you are currently subscribed to? Just because you once had an interest in clothing from the XYZ store doesn't mean you have to stay in touch with them forever. Spend 8 minutes a day until you have finished unsubscribing to sites that no longer interest you. You'd be surprised how this will lighten the load in your inbox.

8 Minutes to Paper Peace

AMBITIOUS 8'S

The time has come for us to get into the nitty-gritty tough projects that abound in any office setup. But have no fear; I've broken even the biggest tasks into chunks you can tackle with ease. Grab a glass of water and your resolve because we're about to dive deep.

Manage Magazine Madness

Make an effort to enjoy your magazines the day they arrive or soon thereafter. Remember that the most current information on just about any topic is on the Internet. You don't have to save a magazine article to be sure that you have the most definitive piece on the subject.

Give yourself a time limit for saving issues. I suggest no more than two months, unless you have a legitimate reason. For example, if you are planning a kitchen remodel, you might collect certain magazines as part of your research. After the project is done, remember to release your research material.

If your profession (such as interior designer, doctor, or attorney) demands that you keep a year's worth of a particular magazine, buy magazine holders designed to sit on a bookcase shelf. You can find holders made from cardboard, plastic, clear acrylic, or wood. You have access to your collection and it takes up little room. Keep your stash in chronological order and buy the holder that goes best with your décor. After you purchase your holders, take 8 minutes to put your magazines in order. Then when the new issue of *Architectural Digest* arrives, you will know where to store it and will be able to easily grab the oldest and recycle it.

I have matching containers for magazines and newspapers. The magazine container is not the type used to hold an entire year's worth of issues; instead, its shape invites browsing. When the new issue of any subscription arrives, I toss the old one. If I haven't made the time to read a magazine over the past one to two months, chances are slim to none I'm going to do so anytime soon.

If you are saving back issues simply out of guilt, let them go. You may have wasted money buying the magazine, but now you're compounding the problem by wasting space. If the number of publications you subscribe to is overwhelming, take 8 minutes to cancel the subscriptions you know you will never have time to read. Shred renewal notices when they arrive in the mail.

Often we buy things just to make ourselves feel better. Do you fall victim to magazine purchases at the supermarket checkout line? Make it a new habit to stop buying magazines while shopping. (You can always ask a friend if you two can swap magazines at month's end.) Then take 8 minutes to set up a system that allows you to track the money you save each day. Buy an old-fashioned piggy bank or use a glass jar and reward yourself for skipping those vices. How much was that magazine you didn't purchase today? Deposit that amount in your home bank. You'll be astonished how much money you can save in a year, and you will get a bonus no purchase can bestow: a sense of pride.

Trust that any information you need will find its way to you or be available to reference on the Internet.

Create Order Out of Catalog Chaos

Gather your catalogs into one area. Hit your timer and, over the next 8 minutes, sort your catalogs into categories and then thin the ranks. How many copies of each catalog do you have? Many are delivered monthly, so the chances are pretty good that you have multiples of your favorites. Be ruthless in tossing. If you absolutely must have a catalog from a particular vendor, keep the most recent and get rid of the rest. As each new edition arrives in the mail, toss the previous one.

When catalogs (as well as business or personal papers and magazines) are stacked, you end up handling only what's at the very top. Counter this by placing your catalogs in a holder that will allow them to stand and face you. Magazine holders (see page 109) or baskets work equally well. If you've been receiving catalogs from particular companies just because you once made a purchase, shoot them an e-mail and ask to be taken off their list. Or mail them a note and enclose your address label, which contains a company code that will make it easier for them to locate your name and delete your information.

Determine Receipts to Retain

After your bills have been whittled down to the mail-in stub, the receipt portion, and the return address envelope and then tucked into your To Do or Bills folder, you might be asking yourself whether you need to keep the receipt portion. The correct answer is: It depends. Receipt retention is essentially dictated by whether or not the expense represents a tax deduction. If the expense is tax deductible, create a folder to keep track of the payments made during the year. At year-end, total the deductions and put the folder away for three to seven years, depending on your tax status. If you can continue to deduct this expense, start a new folder for the next year.

Tax laws change and the person who can best guide you in terms of record retention is the individual you pay to do your return. In general, if you file as an individual, keep your receipts for three years. If you file as a corporation, you need your receipts for seven years. However, these guidelines are only the current federal ones. Each state can dictate a different time period. And because life for the American taxpayer is always complicated, you need to check on specific guidelines for investment receipts and legal documents such as a home purchase. Again, your tax preparer and income tax attorney are your best guides. One of them, not the Zen organizer, will be going with you in the event of an audit.

What will you be doing during these 8 minutes? Look at your checkbook register or your monthly statement (some are more detailed than others) and credit card statements and see which payments are made without fail each month: rent or mortgage payment, utilities, medical insurance, automobile payments, and the like. Make a folder for each type of payment. (If you don't deduct the expense on your taxes, save the receipt in your Pending folder until next month's bill comes in, check that you were credited, and then toss the receipt.)

It shouldn't take more than 8 minutes to set up these file folders. Your file system might look something like this:

- Automobile
- Banking
- Credit cards
- Household expenses
- Investments
- Medical

If your life is more complicated, you might want to sub-divide your categories. Each entry in the preceding list would be the name of a tab on a hanging file folder, and each hanging folder would contain several manila folders inside. This more detailed file system might look like this:

- **AUTOMOBILE** (hanging folder with tab)
  BMW (manila folder)
  Chevy truck (manila folder)

- **BANKING**
  Citibank
  Wells Fargo

- **CREDIT CARDS**
  Capital One: Business
  Capital One: Personal

- **HOUSEHOLD EXPENSES**
  Mortgage
  Repairs
  Utilities
  Landscaping

- **INVESTMENTS**

- **MEDICAL**
  Claim forms
  Medical, Mary
  Medical, Roger

People allow themselves to become overwhelmed by paper as if it had magical properties. However, papers fall into related categories just like the garments in your closet. You don't want to see your blue jeans mixed in with your cocktail dresses, do you? In the same way, you don't want your medical bills tossed in with your utility receipts. Categories, even broad ones, keep you organized. Remember, though, that the file system you create today will be changed over time, with some files added and others deleted. These changes are a good thing! Without movement in your files, you're living a static life.

You don't have to make all your folders at once. Do as many as you can in one 8-minute session and then schedule additional 8-minute sessions until you are done.

Pay Bills on Time

You have several choices for staying on top of your bill paying. Following are some options; feel free to mix and match them as needed:

- Set up automatic payments either directly with the vendor or through your bank. This option saves time but requires that you check the amount each month for computer errors or sudden rate hikes by the vendor. Be sure to note the payment in your check register!
- Set up online bill payments. Simply log in each month and set the amount to be paid and the date. Your bills will arrive by e-mail. Most vendors allow you to set up reminders so you don't forget the due date. Again don't forget to note the amount.
- Pay bills by snail mail on the 1st and the 15th of the month, depending on the due date. Set a reminder on

your computer or in your calendar so you won't forget these important dates.

- Note on your calendar when you need to pay the bill before you file the payment coupon in the Bills or To Do folder in your action files section. You can file the receipt portion in your Pending folder if you need it only until next month or in the appropriate folder if it is a tax-deductible expense.

- Consider hiring a bookkeeper if your bills are complicated. Check the monthly statement, however, to be sure no unexpected expenses or amounts were recorded.

Take 8 minutes to decide how you will handle your bills. Again, this step is critical because timely bill payment is a huge factor in determining your credit score. Then take another 8 minutes to set up your payments. Remember that you aren't stuck with any decision. You can make changes should a system or vendor not respond as you expect.

Create Archives

Income tax receipts are the bulk of the material filling up most file cabinets, but another culprit consists of projects from the past. We save them because they represent a lot of time and devoted energy. The project might be that remodel you did 8 years ago or the research material you're saving from your master's degree. You know, the one you earned 30 years ago? What files from the past are occupying prime real estate in your cabinet?

Round One

Take 8 minutes to open a file drawer and assess the situation. For each project you discover, ask yourself whether you will need to reference the material again:

- If your response is yes, how much longer do you need to keep the material? If you need to keep the information but will rarely if ever access it, pack it for archival storage. Don't bother to sort these files and make them more organized. Devote the time to current files.
- If the response is no, can you recycle or shred the contents? If you want to save pieces of information (for example, names and contact numbers of contractors you used during a remodel), set aside business cards or invoices before you let go of the bulk of the paper.

Round Two

Your old projects and tax backup material may create mounds that must be shredded. If you come up with a box or two of material that needs shredding, don't let it create a longtime eyesore in your office. Spend 8 minutes researching shredding services in your area. If you can take the paper to the service, the shredding is usually inexpensive. Find a service that is both licensed and bonded. (You can ask them to shred the material in your presence.)

Stop Warranty Worries

I bet your warranties and instruction manuals are scattered all over the house or dumped together in a file drawer. When you need to reference one, the quest for the material is arduous. Is there any hope? Of course!

Round One

Take 8 minutes to gather your warranties and manuals. If some elude you, don't worry—you can transfer them to your system as you come across them later.

Round Two

Take another 8 minutes to sort the stacks into related categories. I find the following categories helpful:

- Appliances (stove, refrigerator, and so on)
- Automobiles
- Computer (printer, monitor, and so on)
- Garage
- Entertainment (DVD player, cameras, television sets, and so on)
- Household (vacuum cleaners and so on)
- Jewelry
- Kitchen equipment (mixer and so on)
- Laundry room (washer, dryer, and so on)
- Office equipment (label maker, desk, office chair, and so on)

Your categories will reveal themselves as you sort your material. By the way, as you sort, you will be amazed how much warranty material pertains to items you no longer own—toss, toss, toss!

Round Three

Write your categories on manila file folders and then place these in alphabetical order in box-bottom hanging file folders. The category names should be announced with a long tab on your box-bottom hanging folder. When your plumber comes to your home and asks if you have the booklet that came with your washer, you will be glad you dedicated this time to sorting this material.

Handling Hobbies and Special Interests

We all have areas of personal interest, such as cooking or sports. Whatever your passion, if it comes with a paper trail, you need to have a folder ready to catch that information so it doesn't get lost. If some of this material is in the form of computer files, keep the file names consistent. You don't want finding information to become a memory game.

Spend 8 minutes sorting through the miscellaneous papers pertaining to your interests or hobbies so you can create categories. If the interest has different aspects, create subcategories to make retrieval of specific information easy. For example, recipes generally get tossed into a folder and forgotten because it takes too much time to wade through that huge stack of paper. The whole of anything is overwhelming, but working on individual parts gives you control. Recipes, for example, might be divided into:

- Appetizers
- Main course
- Salad
- Desserts
- Wines

A note for the clippers out there: Be sure you clip only the recipe or article you want. If you save the entire newspaper page or magazine page, you will rapidly add bulk to your file system.

Seek Paper Peace

Instead of seeing an enemy in every piece of paper, you can be the master of your domain (thank you, *Seinfeld*) and instead see a handy helper. After all, the papers that don't find their way to the trash are meant to help you in some way. Dedicate a few 8-minute cycles to creating order and, in less time than you imagine, you will be in charge. You will be able to find documents easily and devote the bulk of your time to more pleasant pursuits. In addition, the time it takes to deal with the unpleasant necessities of life such as taxes will be less frenetic and stressful. Remember that famous Nike ad, and just do it!

FAMILY ROOM MINUTES

Every age that is dying is simply another age coming to life.
—BOETHIUS, a philosopher of fifth-century Rome

The ideal family room is a casual place where everyone gathers throughout the day and shares activities—a "kick back and enjoy" area. But casual doesn't mean the room has to be in constant upheaval. In our 8-minute projects, I'll cover most of the common trouble zones. The issues in this room tend to be the same no matter the location or socioeconomic level of my clients.

Family life, like relationships, is messy, vibrant, and often chaotic. With a little work, you can also make it peaceful, calm, nurturing, and supportive.

The family room most commonly falls into disarray when each person is not responsible for restoring the room to order as he or she leaves. It's not unlike the situation in the bathroom. Sometimes family members don't put things away because the items do not have a designated spot. (Don't worry—the projects in this chapter will establish some rules as to where items can go.)

Your New Family Room Exit Ritual

Having fun in the family room can mean any number of activities, such as listening to music, watching a DVD or television program, playing a computer or board game, or engaging in a hobby. While you're doing any of these activities, you might bring in a snack to enjoy. Your family room exit ritual should be a reversal of every action you take here. As everyone leaves the room, they can do the following:

- Return to the kitchen any food items they brought to the family room.
- Return any item they used for entertainment (DVD, board game, magazine) to its designated spot.
- Return books to a bookcase and toys to waiting bins, where they can be sorted by type (Barbie dolls, G.I. Joe action figures, stuffed toys, and so on). Even young children can do this.
- Turn off electronic equipment and lights.
- Fold any blankets used and fluff the pillows where they sat.

As with many of the other exit rituals, no one has to do every step, every single time. You only have to reverse what you set in motion to complete the process.

Life Tweak

Silence the inner critic. We all engage in mental chatter during the day. For some people with high self-esteem, the chatter is positive. You pass a department store window, catch a glimpse of yourself, and think, "Damn! I look good today!" But for the rest of us mere mortals, that unconscious chatter can be fairly negative. When it comes to getting organized, the negative comments kick into high gear. Suddenly the voice of a friend, family member, or coworker is loud and clear in your head, reminding you of past efforts to get organized. It might sound something like this: "Why are you trying to get organized? You know you were born without the organizing gene. How many times have you tried to do this? You are wasting time and money!" When you hear this monologue, make a conscious decision to stop it midsentence and replace it with a positive affirmation. Perhaps your affirmation will sound something like this: "I am ready to change my life for the better. I deserve to live in a calm, peaceful home that nurtures and supports me. My work begins with the physical state of my home. I am successful at getting organized because I take one step at a time and build on my success." You can repeat this mental action throughout the day. Soon you'll find the negative inner critic will be silent about your organizing efforts.

Extra Ammo

Assign chores to family members and attach consequences when they are ignored, such as loss of privileges and timeouts. If you are a people pleaser by nature, you may find this task difficult at first. Some moms become the de facto maid in the home; if chores are assigned, no one pays attention to them because they know mom will step in and do it all. Other moms are perfectionists. They prefer to do all the tidying because they feel that no one does it faster or better. Both types mean well, but when you expect your children to do chores, you help them learn how to manage a home. In addition, children (and animals) feel more secure when rules, boundaries, and limitations are in place. When those rules, boundaries, and limitations expand over time, children have something to strive for. Start here in the family room with a fluffed pillow, a folded blanket, and a video game that got put away after it was used.

Fresh Eyes Exercise: The Family Room

Walk into this room and have a seat. Look around and see how you feel. You have 8 minutes, so don't be in a rush to judgment. Remember, the goal is to pretend you are here for the first time. What is your impression of this family? Are they a messy bunch? Does the room hold too much stuff? Or do you enjoy the lived-in look of the room, which has a comfortable, not sloppy, vibe?

At the midpoint mark of 4 minutes, make a few notes. What could you do immediately to make this room function better, such as taking out the trash or moving furniture? Can you see any long-term solutions, such as buying new furniture? After you make your list, schedule the long-term items in your calendar.

Speed Elimination: The Family Room

For 8 minutes, you're going to tear around this room looking for obvious items that need to leave. I bet a few glasses or dishes should make their way back to the kitchen. Does a jacket need to be hung in the entry closet? Perhaps some dry cleaning never made it back to your room? If stuff is all over the room, pile it into categories. Now is *not* the time to sort your DVDs, CDs, magazines, or catalogs; instead, eliminate the visual clutter created by the various stacks and piles.

8 Minutes to Family Time

QUICKIES

The family room may be chaotic when you start, so I have a few quickies that will alter the visual dramatically. Sometimes the smallest action can make the biggest difference. Do you doubt me? Just try a brighter bulb by the couch or your favorite easy chair and see how the room becomes a more inviting place to read everything from novels to CD covers.

Round Up the Remotes

The average home has an unconscionable number of remotes. If you can't switch to a Universal remote, employ a basket to hold your collection in one place. I bet the pantry or garage holds an empty basket, such as the one you got flowers in last Valentine's Day. You will no longer hear, "Has anyone seen the remote?" in your home.

Dock Those Devices

Nowadays, "Where is my phone?" is heard almost as frequently as "Where are my keys?" "What did I do with my glasses?" and "Where's the remote?" Create a docking station in the family room and let everyone know where to plug in their phones so they will be charged for the next day. Now both your remotes and your cell phones have a home.

Suck It Up!

Whip out your vacuum cleaner and give the room a quick once-over. A freshly vacuumed room always looks and feels more organized. (Plus, dust in a stuffed room often can cause a sneezing fit when you start to organize the space.) If your family balks at putting things back, you can enforce this rule: Nothing that has an official, designated spot gets left on the floor. If someone is forgetful, the consequence is—you guessed it—vacuuming!

Let There Be Light

In the average home, many rooms have inadequate lighting, making it difficult to see things clearly and easily. Take a few minutes to check out the family room's lighting, especially reading lights and task lights. Should you bring in a few lamps from another room or add lamps to your shopping list? You want to keep your eyes healthy. While you're enjoying the new well-lit landscape, enjoy a raw carrot or two! Might as well support those eyes from the inside out as well.

Switch It Up

Switch out the bulbs in the family room to energy savers. You don't want to be reading, watching TV, or playing computer games in the dark. You'll more than likely be in this room for hours each day, so why not save money in the process?

Say Cheese!

Have you ever been in the middle of a family function when someone yelled, "Can we get a shot of this?" In today's world, cell phones are whipped out and the moment gets captured. Designate a storage spot for your digital camera so that everyone in the family knows where to run to get it—and where to return it. While you're at it, check your camera to be sure the batteries are fresh and the memory card isn't full.

8 Minutes to Family Time

BASIC 8'S

We can see better now; the family room floor is vacuumed and everything is charged. Time to dive in and start clearing some of those pesky items that collect here.

Toss Some Toys

The issue with toys is that we add more without culling those that our children have outgrown. If your children are toddlers, you can do the eliminating for them when they are not in the room. If they are older and will feel violated if they are not consulted (even regarding items they haven't touched in months or years), ask them for their input.

Spend 8 minutes doing a quick clean sweep of this room for toys that need to be tossed or donated. You'll want two sturdy garbage bags at the ready. Soon the room should feel lighter and easier to navigate.

My clients frequently ask their children to do this kind of eliminating not only to make more room in the home but also to help less fortunate children who can't afford to buy new toys. Complete the lesson by having your children accompany you when you drop off the donations.

Toy Round Up

After completing the preceding 8-minute round, the remaining toys are like the clothes in your closet or the papers in your file cabinet: They need to be categorized and housed in a beautiful, functional, and easy-to-maintain way. Toys generally fall into several broad categories: board games, stuffed animals, electronic media, games with many pieces, and collections. Take a moment to look around and decide which categories of toys you have. Now take 8 minutes and make separate piles, isolating the various members of your categories with one exception—electronic media can be a separate project because it tends to be such a huge category in most homes.

After everything is together, sit back and survey the room. Where is the best place to keep each of these categories? Plan to put toys for the younger set in a separate location than those for older siblings. For now, don't worry about how to organize and contain these groups. Just realize what you have and where you'd like it to reside.

Don't Be "Board"

Frequently used board games can be stacked in a built-in cupboard or placed on a bookcase shelf. If the games have small pieces or damaged boxes, stack them. Otherwise, place as many boxes as you can on their sides. Retrieving a game by pulling it out from its place in a line-up of games is easier than lifting a stack of games to get to the one you want. (And it's Murphy's Law that you want the one on the bottom, right?) It shouldn't take more than 8 minutes to set up your board games in tidy stacks and rows. Pop the smaller pieces of popular games into zippered storage bags so that the pieces do not get lost or separated from the game. If the box of a popular game is falling apart, patch it with some masking tape. You can also find heavy-duty generic board game replacement boxes by Googling "Game Saver" boxes.

Store Stuffed Toys

Stuffed toys do well in a bin. Pulling out the toys should be easy—and so should popping them back in place. For the youngest members of the family, a toy bin is a great introduction to the fundamental concepts of getting organized. The old-fashioned toy chest is a wonderful place for stuffed animals, provided you have the floor space and the hinge allows the lid to stay open—you don't want the lid to come crashing down on small fingers.

Pop-up containers in various sizes are great for stuffed animals. You have probably seen them in black and white in the home section of stores such as Bed Bath & Beyond, where they are sold as inexpensive hampers. You can now find them in pastel colors for kids. Another option is a simple big basket. Find a container in your home that you can repurpose or add one to your shopping list.

Putting the stuffed animals away will take about 2 minutes. If you want to have a little fun, place one or two animals so that they appear to be peering out of the container.

Rein in Reading Material

Paper clutter is common in the family room. Newspapers, magazines, mail, school papers abound. Following are some tips to keep these items at bay:

- Keep newspapers in a newspaper holder or basket.
- Place magazines in a holder (preferably one that matches your newspaper container). No matter what the item, you need to keep it confined; otherwise it will proliferate and overwhelm you.
- Move mail and school papers to their designated spot, unless the family room is the place for reading the mail, paying the bills, and completing homework.

The most important tip I can share when it comes to managing paper is to ritualize how you handle it when it comes into your home. Otherwise, you will find yourself constantly searching for that important document, Janie's homework, or the last issue of your favorite magazine.

Decide what types of paper will reside here and where it will be placed. Next, see if you have the necessary containers. If not, put these items on your shopping list. These are quick decisions, so don't be surprised if paper is handled in this room in no time at all.

Make a Move

Take a look at the layout of this room as you currently have it set up. Would it be fun for you and your family to shake things up a bit and move some furniture around? Often, just moving a few items gives the room a new feel that coincides nicely with the new rules that govern how this space is to be used. Move a few things if feasible and see whether the new arrangement supports your efforts to be more organized.

8 Minutes to Family Time

AMBITIOUS 8'S

The next projects are indeed ambitious, so in the spirit of the family room, why not engage a little help? CDs, DVDs, and books inspire passions in people who love music, movies, and reading. Give everyone a chance to participate in the new order. With a sense of ownership, they will be more likely to maintain the order they help create.

Categorize CDs

Some readers have modest collections of music, so organizing their CDs will happen in a flash with minutes to spare. But large families or serious music buffs may be faced with a collection that grows like wildflowers in spring. Every day, new ways of storing music (think iCloud or iTunes for example) come into the marketplace. No matter how you ultimately store your collection, you want to have it organized. This section will give you choices and provide ample food for thought.

Round One

Divide your CD collection by type of music (hip-hop, country western, Broadway, rock 'n' roll, R&B, and so on). If you have a large collection, this task may require several 8-minute segments. Make it a game, not a homework assignment. Work on a stack while running a load of laundry or during commercials of your favorite evening program. If you have a large family and each member favors a different type of music, engage everyone and let them work on organizing their music.

Men generally love to have their music collections in strict alphabetical order. I'm not in favor of this plan for two reasons. Alphabetizing takes a lot of time, and if you purchase CDs frequently, you will forever be moving them to make room for the latest addition. But if the men in the house want to take the time to alphabetize and promise to maintain the order, I say let them have at it!

Round Two

After your collection is sorted, look at the number of CDs in each genre and make the best decision about how to organize them. Here are my favorite options:

- **BOOKCASE SHELF:** Stack your CDs on a bookcase shelf. If you don't have a bookcase, purchase an inexpensive one. I would label the shelves so that family members know exactly where to find a particular genre.
- **BUILT-IN DRAWERS:** Some entertainment units come with built-in drawer organizers for jewel cases. This elegant storage solution keeps your collection out of sight but easy to retrieve.
- **MUSIC HOLDERS:** Some music holders are freestanding while others sit on a shelf of your entertainment unit. These purchases are dictated by the number of CDs you have in a particular genre.
- **BINDERS:** I like to put my collection in binders. You can purchase a utilitarian three-ring binder from Staples or go all out and pick up a leather-bound beauty from a specialty store. There are special inserts for media storage. I get mine at The Container Store. Why do some people break out into a sweat when they hear this choice? Because it means being separated from the jewel case and the colorful information jacket that accompanied the CD. If you are a serious music person and always want to know who is playing the instruments or what the lyrics of the song are, this choice might not be right for you. This solution is the most compact solution of all the previous options. Next up, the biggest space-saver of all.

- **DIGITAL STORAGE:** The most popular choice is to keep your music on your iPod or MP3 player and put the CDs in storage in the event you might want to sell them one day or need to reload the music should you lose your iPod.

Read these suggestions and perhaps have a family discussion about them. What solution will work best for everyone? After all, if you set up a system that no one will honor, you've wasted your time.

Divide the DVDs

The instructions for organizing your DVDs are like the ones for CD organization. The big hurdle is creating categories. Most people categorize along these lines: comedies, dramas, documentaries, and so on. Again, binders and sleeves are my favorite space-saving option.

Move the Media

If an electronic entertainment collection threatens to overtake a room, why not take some of the collection to your bedroom? The kids are not likely to be interested in your music or romantic comedies, and you probably don't care too much for their music, games, or action flicks. And your children may prefer playing computer games in their room, alone or with a best buddy. It's okay to split a collection so that some selections stay in the room where they will be enjoyed.

Create a Reading Room

I grew up with a mother who read to me every night and

passionately believed the proverb "A house without books is like a house without windows." The problem for some readers, however, is that they ultimately have so many books that they live in homes made of glass. Well, you get the idea, right? Let's work to tame those unruly, sprawling, space-sucking collections into a home library that everyone can enjoy. Along the way, you may decide that some members of your collection can be shared with friends, family members, the library, or your local shelter or hospital. And don't forget two popular websites: Paper Back Swap and Free Cycle. Where there's a will, there's a website.

Round One

Take 8 minutes to look around this room at your book collection and decide the fate of your various categories. Spend this time making notes rather than getting up and frantically moving books around without a plan.

Do you realize now that some books belong in your child's room while others should be moved to another room in the home? Can any books be donated to a charity, such as Goodwill, or your local library? If your family room is large, could the room accommodate several bookcases?

You don't need to limit your bookcase to published books. Too often we make photo albums or scrapbooks and tuck them away where no one can see them. Instead, consider putting them on a bookshelf so that guests and family can go down memory lane. And in this age of electronic readers, you might want to include an e-reader charging station on the top of the bookcase.

Round Two

Take 8 minutes to divide your collection by genre and destination. Separate those books that belong elsewhere and that you want to donate. Move quickly. Don't be concerned with organizing each category. Don't create overly complicated systems. Don't bother with alphabetical order. Do keep categories together on a shelf and vary the visuals (page 28). If you have several children, dedicate a shelf to each child, with the bottom shelf reserved for the youngest one's books.

At the end of this round, transfer or return books that belong elsewhere in the house and pack up the ones you want to donate.

Round Three

Now take 8 minutes to make your bookcases look inviting. You may need extra time if you are a voracious reader with an extensive collection. Decide whether you want to add decorative items to the display or if you want more of a library feel. Stand up books that you are most likely to grab. Stack the reference material and coffee table books. Vary the placement style on each shelf (page 28). And don't be afraid of space—leave room for future purchases.

BUY IT: SCRAPBOOK CONTAINERS

Scrapbooking stores and online sites have containers designed for the unique needs of this hobby. Take a look at some of the containers suggested here for other purposes. Items such as acrylic shoe drawers and grid totes will serve you well.

Collect Craft Supplies

Do you create beautiful photo albums and scrapbooks? Is sewing your passion? Whatever your crafty endeavor, the family room can be ideal for this type of work, but you may prefer to share space in the home office so you can get away and work on your hobby in private.

Round One

Take 8 minutes to survey the supplies you have and consider how much time you want to devote to this hobby. Is there space in the family room, or do you have to set up elsewhere? Or are your hours of scrapbooking over and it is now time to pack up your supplies and put them in storage or pass them on to a friend? Some hobbies are forever, but others last only a few seasons.

Round Two

After your supplies are organized and accessible (perhaps on a bookcase shelf), you will certainly need a table or desk. You might want to use a card table, but if you have to break it down each time you are ready to exit the family room, I think you'll find your hobby becoming less important to you.

Some of my clients prefer to go to craft or scrapbook stores to work on their projects and have specially designed cases on wheels for all their supplies. If this is your choice, do you have everything tucked neatly into your case? Do you store it in this room or in the hall closet? Take 8 minutes and create a plan. For example, you'll want to know which items will live in your traveling bag and which items will stay in your hobby area at home.

Do you need any special storage containers? What's the state of your supplies? When you can't find a key element, you can't enjoy your hobby. Moreover, you might fall into the trap of constantly buying new gizmos and supplies but never having the time or place to actually use them. Everybody deserves to have a hobby that fosters their creativity and brings them escape from the mundane details of everyday life. And that hobby deserves a place of respect in your home.

Crop Your Photo Collection

The family room is often chock-full of framed family photos. Are so many photos crowding this room that it's impossible to appreciate them? Is the collection so heavy with baby photos that your teenagers don't want their dates to go into this room? Remember that photos should be a conscious addition to a room's décor.

Round One

Take your 8 minutes to view your collection and decide which photos can be eliminated from this room. You may want some photos to go into an album so that the frame can be used for a newer photo. You might even keep all your photos on display but move them into different positions or groupings around the room. Small shifts like this make big changes in the way the room appears and feels.

Round Two

Following are some quick ideas to help break the photo stalemate:

- Put the oldest photos in a large envelope; add them to a photo album at a later date.
- Reduce your photos by half and rotate them. Divide them in categories, such as seasonal, school events, or milestones. It's fun to remember old Halloween costumes in the fall or see images from the summer family reunions when it starts to get warm. You get the idea.
- Designate a single, contained location for photos instead of allowing them to take up every surface in the family room and beyond.

Use this time to consider a more effective photo display of your family's history. Rather than letting photos just explode on walls and surfaces over time, be in charge of the story you want to tell.

After you have chosen a solution, decide how many steps it will take to make the transition and then grab your calendar and schedule the time. Working in 8-minute segments, you will make the changes in no time!

Preserving Children's Artwork

Who doesn't love his or her child's artwork? If you must save it all, designate a storage area for it—such as a large plastic bin. At the end of the school year, ask your child to choose the two best pieces, and store those in an artist's portfolio. (You can find inexpensive ones at The Container Store.) Clearly mark the school year and your child's age on the outside. As for the rest of your child's artwork, if you must preserve them, take digital snapshots and create a free scrapbook online at www.snapfish.com. Now Uncle

Murray, your parents, and your best friend from college can see your little one's work and progress over the years. Simply photograph the artwork throughout the year. Remember, though, that it is okay to let most of the pieces go. I've never met an adult who had any of his or her childhood artwork up on the walls!

A Fun Family Room

I stopped at a friend's house one day to pick her up for an event. Her three teenage children—along with their friends who had stayed overnight—had trashed the family room. When my friend told me she couldn't leave until order had been restored to the room, I thought that we were going to be late. I went to the bathroom to primp after my long ride to her house, and when I came out about 5 minutes later, the room looked perfect. I couldn't believe my eyes. But then I realized that everyone had simply pitched in and returned each stray item to its designated spot, folded the blankets, and fluffed the pillows. I saw the power of placement in action. Your family room can be restored in minutes as well. Just make sure to ask everyone to be responsible for his or her own mess. I think that's fair. Don't you?

7
KIDS' ROOM MINUTES

Welcome the present moment as if you had invited it.
Why?
Because it is all we ever have.

—PEMA CHÖDRÖN

A child's room is his or her castle. Children learn how to take care of their future home in this room. Is your child set up to win, or have you thrown your hands up in frustration at the state of your child's bedroom? My best advice is to model in your bedroom how you want your children to live in their rooms. Gandhi said it best: "You must be the change you wish to see in the world." Too often, parents will call me to their homes to organize their children while their own rooms look like a cyclone just blew through. This "do as I say, not as I do" school of parenting is not effective. If you are reading this chapter out of sequence, be sure you have worked on your own bedroom first. Ultimately you can make every aspect

141

of your bedroom so inviting, organized, peace filled, and calm that your kids will want to emulate you.

Life Tweak

Even young children can do four daily things in their room:

- Make the bed
- Keep related items together
- Use a hamper
- Check the trash

Make the Bed
The bed needn't look like an ad for Ralph Lauren's home collection. In fact, you can skip the top sheet and give your child a washable duvet cover to simply pull and smooth into place. You'll be making *your* bed each day, so the example will be set.

Keep Related Items Together
Boxes and bins come in many sizes and shapes. Designate bins (at kid level) for different types of toys and then teach your child where they go. Even young children toss stuffed animals, blocks, and Barbies in the correct bin. Help young children learn to separate their belongings into different bins, and later their video games, homework, and hobby equipment will all be kept in separate zones.

Use a Hamper
Wet towels and dirty clothing don't belong on the floor

when a designated hamper can catch them. You may be doing your kids' laundry, but you don't have to be their maid!

Check the Trash

If your child is too young to empty the trash, have him or her be the monitor who lets you know when it needs to be emptied.

Extra Ammo

If your children are old enough to do laundry, teach them to launder their own sheets, towels, and clothing. When they go off to college or get their first apartment, they'll be self-sufficient in this all-important area. Very young children love to help, so let them pour in the detergent, add the dryer sheet, and set the dials.

Fresh Eyes Exercise: The Kid's Room

Walk into your child's room and pretend that you have never been here before. Doing so can be an eye-opening experience, perhaps the most powerful you will have in any area of your home. For most parents, the big discovery is that toys and clothing from another era in the child's life fill the environment. When parents tell me their children don't spend a lot of time in their rooms, I know why the minute I enter: The past has taken hold of the space. The items they have outgrown physically and emotionally need to leave the room. Allow your children to have adequate space for the toys, clothing, and hobbies that interest them today. Often the parent, not the child, is still attached to certain items in this room.

Walk into your child's room and see what you discover. Here some things to look for that cover various ages and interests:

- Is the room generally messy or tidy? Do the children have chores and responsibilities in their room, or do you or a housekeeper keep it clean?
- Could any toys they have outgrown be donated to a charity or passed on to the child of a friend or relative?
- Do the closet and drawers hold clothing that is no longer worn? Is it time to go shopping?
- Does the room hold too many pieces of furniture, or does it need, say, a dresser to be more functional?
- Does the closet need some tools to make it work better? Whatever you used in your bedroom organization will work well here.
- If homework is done in this room, is the area set up to support strong academic achievement?
- Do you allow your child to have friends over? Is there adequate seating and lighting?

Make notes about what you see and then schedule a time to make the improvements. If your children are old enough, get their input and ask for their help. But remember that the key phrase is "old enough." A fine line exists between not respecting your children and overwhelming them with decisions that they are too young to make.

One last caveat: Children aren't adults in small packages. They aren't born fully coordinated, so they spill things and break things. They have to learn how to take care of their possessions. Don't spend a fortune on high-end furniture and top-of-the-line organizing tools: Shop somewhere between Neiman Marcus and a thrift store. That way, if something happens to these purchases, you won't have a coronary.

Speed Elimination: The Kid's Room

Time for a speed elimination, which you may want to do with your child. If your children are in their late teens, they can do their own speed elimination. Set your timer for 8 minutes and see how many things you can eliminate from the space. Have two sturdy garbage bags: one for trash and one for donations.

Eliminating is at the heart of being organized, and these 8 minutes will enable your child to learn the skill with you. However, ask another adult to do the speed elimination with your child if you know that you are attached to certain items and will be saying, "Are you *sure* you don't want that?" Otherwise, all your child learns is that eliminating is an emotional experience and it is best to hang on to everything.

8 Minutes Closer to a Clean Room

QUICKIES

You will recognize some of these quickies from your time organizing your bedroom. Now you know firsthand what a big difference they make. Your children have seen these changes in your closet and, depending on their age, may feel quite grown-up seeing a similar transformation in their space.

Banish Plastic

One of the fastest ways to see a change in the environment and gain space in the process is the exercise we did in your closet. Remove all plastic from the dry cleaners. This task won't take long and will make a big difference in your child's closet space. You also instill a sense of accomplishment coming out of the starting gate. Let your child do the rip, tear, and toss!

BUY IT: ORGANIZERS FOR TOYS

Try an over-the-door canvas shoe bag for small toys. Alternatively, check your local home store for a larger canvas holder that attaches to a closet rod with Velcro and creates a series of shelf-like pockets for storing items such as T-shirts and sweats. Who says it has to hold clothing? Use it for storing lightweight toys.

Whisk Away Wire

Yes, those horrific wire hangers I asked you to eliminate from your closet must also exit your child's closet (and your guest and coat closets as well). Inexpensive plastic tubular hangers, scaled down to fit small garments, work well. When your child graduates to adult-size clothes, you can invest in more expensive hangers, like yours. If your son or daughter has a few special outfits, pick up some child-size padded hangers to preserve the integrity of the fabric.

Order Outfits

Is a fashionista born or made? If your children can't grasp what makes an outfit, hang a selection of outfits together where they can reach them. By combining appropriate tops and bottoms (not to mention color matches and blends), you'll be educating your children while helping them get organized and save time. Now, that's what I call multitasking!

Create Photo Labels for Bins

If your children are too young to read, take a photo of the type of toy you'd like in each container and then attach each photo to its respective bin. With a digital camera and a printer, you'll have your image in seconds. And if you happen to have a laminator at home, you can create a long-lasting label. Punch a hole in the label and attach it to the bin with string, a pretty ribbon, or dental floss. You can use this technique elsewhere. Take a photo of a type of clothing and attach it to the drawer where those items reside. Use this technique in the bathroom and kitchen, especially if your child is visual by nature.

Start Saving

We're living in a consumer-driven age, so I'm fairly certain your children have a long list of items they need because their buddies have this stuff. Why not encourage them to earn money by doing extra chores? Turn a container into a makeshift bank. Decide which item your child could conceivably earn the money to purchase and designate this jar as the Transformer, iPod, or Xbox savings bank. When your child has enough saved, you can both go shopping. We all like gifts, but the things we earn raise our self-esteem and sense of appreciation.

8 Minutes Closer to a Clean Room

BASIC 8'S

In this round, we tackle several of my favorite projects for kids. None is more important than streamlining the backpack. Let's get started.

Unpack the Backpack

Super-heavy backpacks can harm your children's developing bone structure. Sit down with them and go through their backpacks to see whether they are transporting items that could be left at home or in the school locker. Check the backpack every month. It's amazing what migrates back into a backpack (or a briefcase, handbag, or tote bag).

Contain a Backpack's Contents

While you're relieving your children's backpacks of un-necessary weight, you also have a wonderful opportunity to teach them the power of categories. Look at the various items your children need to transport, and ask them if they can spot related items. Then go shopping with your children and purchase containers they will enjoy using; otherwise, the containers will be abandoned and the mess will continue. While you are buying simple zippered mesh bags to organize your purse, your children might select the Hello Kitty, Star Wars, or Barbie version for their writing implements.

Use Kid-Friendly Linens

Most parents have two sets of sheets for their children, one on the bed and the other in the linen closet. For the extra sheet set, keep the fitted sheet and the top sheet (if you're using one) inside the pillowcase so that the linens stay together. A tip: Assign a specific color for each child's sheet set and towels. And you thought color organizing was only for files and clothing!

Show your child how to strip and then make the bed from scratch. The process won't take your child more than 8 minutes and will save time and avoid aggravation, espe-cially if your household includes several children.

Make Cleanup a Game

When your child is young, have 8-minute speed-clean sessions that are presented as a game or something to be enjoyed. Don't be too rigid. The bookcase doesn't have to be ready to be photographed for the Pottery Barn Kids catalog. Just make sure that related toys are together. Be happy if books are on a bookcase shelf and toy parts are in related bins.

Following are the basics of toy storage:

- Sort different types of toys in sturdy, washable bins.
- Put stuffed animals in their own bin, with a few left out to decorate a bed.
- Shelve books in the bookcase.
- Use smaller bins that fit on a shelf for toys with multiple parts. When your child outgrows these types of toys, the "bin shelf" can store additional books.
- Use small zippered storage bags to keep small pieces together.
- Supply storage solutions for DVDs and video games, as you did in the family room, if your child's room has a small TV, computer, or video game console.

8 Minutes Closer to a Clean Room

AMBITIOUS 8'S

You're on a roll now and there's no stopping you. What makes you feel like a grown-up? That's right: dressing yourself. And what lets you know you're getting older? That's right: homework. Let's make both a littler easier.

Tame Clothing Chaos

Your child's closet can be patterned after yours when it comes to organization (see page 36). Children's wardrobes are usually smaller than adults (literally and in the number of clothes), so you'll have only a few 8-minute projects in this room.

Round One
If your children are too young to reach the closet pole, install a low-hanging bar so they can make choices about what they want to wear. Keep fancy clothes up high. If you have a built-in closet system, adding a bar is easy. If you have an old-fashioned closet, you can purchase a closet rod and install it.

Round Two
The easiest project is switching out old hangers to have a uniform set.

Round Three
Now that your children's closet contains new hangers, take one 8-minute segment to divide the clothing by type and then by color. In addition, consider reversing the usual order in the child's dresser, with socks and underwear in low drawers that the child can reach.

Avoid Bathroom Brawls
You know what's coming: the kids' bathroom will be organized just like yours.

Round One
Consider the following quick organizing initiatives:

- Line the drawers and use drawer organizers from the time baby comes home from the hospital. The items inside will change, but order will be part of the land-scape from day one.

- Make sure the room has enough hooks, bars, and shelves.
- Purchase a one-step step stool suited for young children.
- Use grid totes. Older children who have lotions and potions can contain them in grid totes; two easy movements and the container is taken out and put away. If more than one child shares a bathroom, use different colored totes to visually separate possessions. Grid totes can be kept in the child's room and brought into the bathroom if this room lacks space for personal storage.
- If the bathroom is in demand, create a schedule for bathroom time during the early morning rush.

If your children are older, include them in a conversation about what will and won't work in the bathroom.

Round Two
A big hurdle to an organized bathroom is clearing out excess products (see page 79). You can do that in one or more separate sessions with your child or let your child do it alone if he or she is old enough.

Round Three
After you shop for any missing tools or containers, spend 8 minutes putting your new purchases to work. Children young and old will enjoy this process.

Help with Homework

Ancient yogis suggested that you meditate in the same place every day. They found the energy of meditation would grow strong in that area and that you would be drawn to that space on the days you were reluctant to meditate. I believe that this philosophy applies to other areas we dedicate to specific activities, including home-work.

Round One

Take 8 minutes to view the spot where your children do their homework. Are you and your spouse in the back-ground discussing the day while making dinner? Is a tod-dler at their feet begging them to play? Do older siblings have the TV blasting in the next room? Consider changing the room where homework is done. If this change is not possible, think about what you can do to enhance the ex-perience. Your list might include the following:

- Additional lamps
- Brighter or higher-wattage bulbs
- An adequate-sized desk and a comfortable chair
- Headphones for the TV or music so others can enjoy their entertainment during homework-designated hours
- Files and binders for keeping track of paper

Round Two

After 8 minutes of critical planning, devote another 8 to working out a plan with your children. Ask what bothers them about the homework area. Tell them about the changes you'd like to make and get their input. If you need to, schedule a shopping trip on your calendar or spend another 8 minutes doing some online shopping for the area in question.

Create Order with Folders and Binders

Are your child's school papers scattered all over? Consider which of the following solutions would work for your child:

- **A COLORED FOLDER FOR EACH SUBJECT OR PROJECT:** When you're working on more than one project, it can be helpful to know what color file you're searching for on your desk.
- **LARGE BINDERS:** Use tabs to divide the subjects and a three-hole punch or sheet protectors to keep the papers in the binder. Your child can create a label for the spine or use different color binders to indicate different subjects.
- **PROJECT BOXES:** This solution is one of last resort because it's pricey. Children who are flummoxed by binders and files can keep material in project boxes. Label the boxes and store them on a shelf.

Take one 8-minute session to talk to your child about these alternatives. After you make your purchases, spend another 8-minute session helping your child put the system together. They will use their newfound skill when they are adults working in an office or helping their own children with homework.

Your Kids' New Bedroom Exit Ritual

Because children should have different responsibilities at different ages, coming up with one exit ritual is difficult. Following are the general steps to teach; you can tweak them as needed:

- Make the bed every day.
- Hang clothing up after it's worn or place it in the hamper.
- Put all toys, books, and other items back in their designated spots.
- Remove all food items; they invite the creepy crawlies.
- Check the trash can and empty it if it is full.
- Turn off the lights.

Yes, this list mirrors the bedroom ritual I suggested you follow! These quick tasks are, as always, about practicing completion.

The Bottom Line

Just before she turned 50, a client of mine went back to school to learn a new profession. She and her 10-year-old son did homework together each evening at the dining room table. Imagine how inspired her son was to see his mother doing homework with him. She not only modeled good homework skills but also showed by example that you can always change the direction of your life.

A child learns how to be organized by observing you. If you are following these guidelines, as your children grow up they will practice what they see in their own space. Provide guidance, the right tools, and as much freedom as their age and maturity level allow.

When it comes to the projects in this chapter, you have to decide how many are best done by you, with your children, or by your children alone. And finally, as children get older, they outgrow clothing, toys, and items of interest faster than adults do. You will also have to make adjustments as time goes on. But remember to enjoy the journey. In a flash, they'll be out of the house for good.

8 THE POWER OF LISTS

Achieving genuine happiness
may require bringing about
a transformation in your outlook,
your way of thinking,
and this is not a simple matter.
    —H.H. THE DALAI LAMA

Being organized can up your happiness quotient. Getting there just requires some changes—the "same old, same old" simply won't produce new and different results. You can take three solid actions toward becoming an organized person: make quick decisions, complete any action you set in motion, and monitor your negative inner chatter. But you have another tool at your disposal: The humble list can transform your organizing experience.

I used to have a photographic memory, so I understand if many of you feel that list making is a waste of time because you have all the key information of your life in your head. Although a good memory is a gift, it may not always be as sharp as it is now—sleep deprivation, pregnancy, aging, or illness are common culprits. Why not simply start writing things down? You won't be as disappointed later if your memory starts to fail.

This chapter is dedicated to the people who are totally lost when it comes to keeping track of their schedule. Imagine driving across the country with a kick-ass map that you never once consult. By navigating on instinct, we waste time making pointless detours. Everyone should know how to create three basic lists: a daily to-do list, a shopping list before heading for the stores, and a packing list before taking a trip. Why lament the things you forgot to do today, stumble around the grocery store mumbling, "I just know there was something else I needed," or haul a huge suitcase? A good list—and knowing how to use it—will help you be more productive and save money, time, and energy.

Everybody makes lists, of course, but they often aren't used in the right way. A list is meant to be a guide. Simply committing the words to paper does not cause anything to happen but is the first step toward action.

Life Tweak

During the day, we frequently make mental notes of minor things we must accomplish. Because we've acknowledged these items so many times, a part of us feels that we have actually completed the tasks. From now on, when you pass a plant that needs water, shoes that need to be returned to your closet, a bird that needs seed, or anything that takes less than a minute and is easy to do, remember the great Nike ad campaign and just do it!

Tie Your List to Your Calendar

A critical part of using lists effectively is to create your to-do list for the next day from notations on your calendar. Making an endless list that never gets tended to or has no real relationship with your life goals is pointless. Your calendar is where you plot the course.

Create a fresh to-do list each day. If new items crop up during the day that you need to enter on your calendar later, jot them down on the back of today's to-do list. When you get home, decide where those items best fit in your current schedule. Also check your purse, briefcase, and pockets for any appointments to log. You will feel in control of the flow of information in your life.

These steps will not take more than 8 minutes. They are not only quick and easy but also afford a measure of comfort and control. Can I say that often enough? You will no longer feel like a chicken with its head cut off, running here and there.

Some of you may be shocked to learn that I don't use Google Calendar, Outlook, or the calendar in my smartphone. Those are wonderful choices (and it's true that my Blackberry is practically surgically attached to my hand), but I prefer my old-fashioned paper Day Runner. The key point is to use the calendar religiously, so use the one that most appeals to you.

Whether your calendar comes from a tree or is on an electronic screen, be sure you enjoy using it. To make any calendar work, you must input information and reference it. The only other solution is a crackerjack personal assistant; but if you don't understand how he's functioning, your life will come to a grinding halt when he gets the flu or quits his job.

Feel Free to Change

Remember that no matter what you write in your calendar, it's okay to make changes. If I have an especially exhausting session with a client, I might bump grocery shopping and laundry a day so I can have some quiet time. Change is okay. If you get into a rigid mindset, you will be setting yourself up for failure. But do watch out for those items that continuously get bumped from one day to the next.

Keep a Bird's Eye View

Another way people get tripped up with calendars is by writing every single thing they need to do in the tiniest space possible. Use a system that gives you some space and don't write down every detail of an appointment. For example, suppose you are managing the remodeling of your entire home. In your calendar, you note on September 10th at 11 a.m.: "Meet with contractor at the house." This isn't the place to list everything you want to discuss with him. Keep your detailed notes in a Home Remodel To Do folder, either a physical folder or a folder on your computer.

Fresh Eyes Exercise: The To-Do List

The to-do list is not only the most important list to master but also the prototype for all other lists. I'd like you to take 8 minutes and write down in columns everything you would like to accomplish in the next week.

When you have finished compiling your list, take a break. Hang up the dry cleaning, feed the dog, tidy up the family room, do something for 8 minutes that's unrelated to list making. Don't think about the list. Creating these lists is a hot-button issue for most people, so be sure a tall glass of water is next to you when you return. Come back to the list with a fresh mind.

For the final 8 minutes, look at your list as though it belongs to someone else. What do you think about this person? Do they seem to live a balanced life? Or do you get the feeling that the person must be bionic because no mere mortal could complete all these tasks in a week? Examine the list even more closely and ask yourself if the bulk of the tasks are busywork or directed toward fulfilling a purpose. You'd be surprised how we fritter away time believing we're being good stewards of it because we're in perpetual motion. Movement and productivity are two separate entities.

Look over the list without negative judgment. If your list is balanced and focused, be proud! That reaction is the goal; if you hit the mark the first time out, you deserve a pat on the back. If your inner critic gets released, put that evil genie back in the bottle. Either way, let's hone our list-making skills even further.

Speed Elimination: The To-Do List

Every first list I have asked my clients to create was filled with unrealistic tasks, such as "organize entire house this weekend" or "learn how to play the piano" (while raising small children and working full time). Mind you, these goals are not impossible. However, the first has to be broken down into projects and spread out over time, and the second might have to wait until the children are older or the person no longer works full time. My goal is never to squash dreams. If you, too, wrote down such currently out-of-reach tasks, you are wasting time and paper and no doubt making yourself feel guilty. For this chapter's speed-elimination, you will whittle your to-do list in two ways: by transferring items to a wish list and by delegating.

We all have things we'd like to do or investigate some-day but can't find the time to do in our daily lives. These "wish list" entries are important, but they don't belong on your daily to-do list. In the back of your calendar, dedicate a page to your wish list and transfer these items there for now. Check your wish list periodically, perhaps on the first of each month, to see whether you are ready to transfer an item to your to-do list and do the work necessary to bring it to fruition. If the status of an item on your wish list changes to "who am I kidding?," remove it with a sigh of relief and nary a tinge of guilt. You're freeing up time and energy for the important things in your life.

Another speed-elimination trick is to delegate them on your to-do list. Following are typical tasks that kids can easily accomplish, provided they are old enough to assume the responsibility. What would you add to my list?

- Water the plants
- Feed the fish
- Feed the cat and the dog and check for fresh water at least twice a day
- Walk the dog
- Make a meal
- Take out the trash and recycling

Plus, if the young person is old enough to drive, there's no end to the errands he or she could run: shop for groceries, pick up the dry cleaning, drop books at the library, mail packages at the post office, and on and on.

You can post weekly chores and shift them on a regular basis. One of my clients has a weekly chore chart. Her children do not receive money for these chores because they are considered the work the children do as family members. However, she has a second chore list dedicated to tasks that her children can perform to earn extra money. Let me just say that her silver is always polished! What about your spouse or partner? Perhaps you don't have children but realize that you are shouldering the bulk of the home duties. Have a calm conversation and see what changes can be made. No one at home to help? Perhaps it makes sense to hire part-time help, a cleaning service, or a virtual assistant—an independent contractor with administrative skills. (You can find virtual assistants online; start with a Google search. Think of a virtual assistant as a Gal or Guy Friday who helps your life run more smoothly. The only tweak is that you will probably never meet your virtual assistant in person because he or she probably lives in another part of the globe.)

As the length of your to-do list diminishes, you will feel more relieved, relaxed, and empowered. You'll have more energy for the remaining items that rightfully belong to you to accomplish.

By the way, a perk comes with making your calendar part of your daily planning. When someone asks if you can do something and you know you want to say no but need time to craft an elegant negative response, simply say, "Oh! I have to check my calendar. Let me get back to you." And that means you don't have to whip out your smartphone and fill every open slot with the requests of others. Give yourself time to consider the validity of the request. Maybe you need that time to rest, read, or do paperwork.

On Your Mark, Get Set, Schedule!

You have a choice, depending on how you feel about your list at this point. If you feel ready, take out your calendar and schedule the items on your current list. If you still feel a bit overwhelmed, determine your categories (such as work, family, recreation) and divide your list accordingly before you enter the items in your calendar. This preliminary step will enable you to see whether one area of life (traditionally, work) is top heavy while another (fun, recreation, family, or spiritual pursuits) is in need of a boost. You'll probably need all 8 minutes for this part.

Rearrange, Recharge, and Redo

Take a look at your calendar and see how "geographically intelligent" you were. Are you returning to the same neighborhood several times a week when you could go to the dry cleaner, grocery store, and pet store in one well-planned visit?

Are you experiencing a particularly difficult time at work now? Schedule some downtime, whether it's a night out with friends or a weekend for kicking back around the house. Do you have a shopping trip planned because of an upcoming birthday, wedding, or graduation? Why not save gas and time by shopping online?

Take a few minutes to examine your schedule rather than just accept it. What changes can you make? Consider any opportunity to eliminate items on your list. Not every category will apply to you, but you want to take full advantage of the exploration. Eventually you will whip through your list in minutes, making it refined, specific, and a true asset.

Make Scheduling a Habit

Right about now, some of you are screaming that all these 8-minute sessions just on the to-do list take too much time! Initially, streamlining your to-do list and working with your calendar *do* take time. Developing any new skill always requires a time investment. But the more you practice scheduling your list in tandem with your calendar, the easier it becomes to make quick, critical decisions. You will automatically protect your need for play time and recovery time and realize when you can take on more. As with all tasks, working on a to-do list requires 21 consecutive days before it becomes second nature. Taking the steps to create the life you want is time well spent.

You may also discover something shocking the first time you do this exercise: You actually have more time at your disposal than you imagined. You may be running so fast and so far from what you want to accomplish that your life is filled with nonessential errands. A scheduled to-do list is more than a random collection of items. A well-thought out schedule list is like a map guiding us to goal fulfillment and helping us keep our lives on track.

Master the Shopping List

Anything in the pantry? You will always be able to answer yes to this question if you have a handy shopping list at the ready and teach everyone in your home to use it. Too often, we wander into the grocery store with a vague idea of what we need and a faint memory of the items we are running low on.

Grab your computer keyboard (preferable for this task) and set your timer for 8 glorious minutes of food fantasy. (If you have a big list, this project might require two 8-minute segments.) Create a list of the items you shop for regularly. The list should be as comprehensive as possible, but it's okay if you don't remember every single item right now.

The easiest way to complete this task is to create food categories and leave space under each category to enter by hand other items you need that week. Print your list, and all you have to do is circle, check, or highlight the item that's needed. Later, you can go back to your master shopping list on the computer and add those handwritten items. Eventually, you'll have a fully comprehensive shopping list tailored to your family's needs.

Find creating your own list daunting? Google *shopping lists* and you'll find a wealth of options in the form of pre-made grocery shopping lists. You can copy and paste them into a word-processing document and tailor them to suit individual needs.

Depending on the size of your family, the number of guests in any given week, and how much you enjoy cooking and baking, you can create a shopping list in one or two 8-minute segments. Create your list on the computer so you can easily print copies on demand and adjust the list as time goes on.

Here's an example list to get you started—see which categories your family would delete or add.

Beverages
- Beer
- Coffee
- Hard liquor
- Soda
- Tea

- Water
- Wine

Food Items
- Breads
- Cereals
- Condiments and spices
- Dairy
- Desserts
- Eggs
- Frozen foods
- Fish
- Fruit
- Meat
- Nuts
- Packaged products
- Poultry
- Produce
- Salad
- Salad dressings

Nonfood Items
- Cleaning supplies
- Kitchen supplies
- Medicines
- Pets
- Toiletries

If I filled in the categories, my list might look like the following. How would you adjust this for your family's tastes and needs?

BEVERAGES

Beer	Coffee	Hard Liquor
Budweiser	Decaf	Gin
Coors	French roast	Scotch
Schlitz		Vodka

Sodas	Tea	Water
Coke	Black	Flat
Pepsi	Chamomile	Sparkling
Root Beer	Green	

Wine

Red
Rose
White

FOOD ITEMS

Breads	Cereals	Condiments and Spices	
English muffins	Corn flakes	Catsup	Basil
Rice Tortillas	Rice Krispies	Mayonnaise	Mint
Rye bread	Wheaties	Mustard	
Whole wheat bread		Pepper	
		Salt	

Dairy	Desserts	Eggs
Butter	Cakes	Fertile
Half and half	Cookies	Cage free, brown
Milk (skim, 2%, whole)	Pies	Cage free, white, large

Frozen Foods	Fruits	Meats
Mixed veggies	Apples	Ground beef
Prepared meals	Bananas	Steaks
	Cherries	

Nuts	Packaged Products
Cashews	Beans
Pistachios	Pasta
Walnuts	Rice

Poultry	Produce
Chicken: Breasts, thighs, whole, wings	Carrots
	Celery
Turkey: Breast, ground, legs	Onions
	Potatoes

Salad	Salad Dressings
Cucumbers	Blue cheese
Greens	Ranch
Jicama	Thousand island
Tomatoes	

NON-FOOD ITEMS

Cleaning Supplies*	Kitchen Supplies	Medicines
Comet	Aluminum foil	Aspirin
Detergent: dish, laundry	Baggies	Band-Aids
Paper towels	Wax paper	Cough syrup
Soap	Trash bags	Windex

Toiletries	Pets
Dental care	Biscuits
Deodorant	Dried food
Feminine hygiene	Toys
Hair care	

*Consider making your own cleaning products. At the New York Times–run website About.com, you can find easy-to-follow recipes that are cheaper than purchased cleaning products and better for the environment.

Polish Your Packing List

So you are planning a trip—what's in your suitcase? If you are like most travelers, the answer is everything but the kitchen sink! I love to travel and have lived out of suitcases off and on since I was 17. My first flight was 11½ hours from New York to Rio, and I lugged not one but two of the biggest, heaviest suitcases you could imagine. Since then, I've learned how to travel the world with a suitcase that holds everything I need and fits in the overhead bin of an aircraft. The two key ingredients to packing light are a list and the ability to learn from inevitable mistakes. Too often, mistakes are seen as personal flaws and an opportunity to browbeat ourselves. Zen organizing will have none of that!

The big travel mistake is taking way more than you'll need. Why do we fall prey to this error over and over again? We pack to feed the uncertain emotions rising inside us as we contemplate the trip. So we start packing multiple outfits, just in case, and toss in every lotion, potion, gadget, and trinket for good measure. All that stuff provides a buffer between us and the fear. Irrational fear robs us of the ability to make good decisions, and we consequently eat too much, drink too much, or, in some cases, pack too much!

Please take 8 minutes to read the following material. Compare these suggestions to how you prepared for your most recent trip. First up, a series of questions designed to help you narrow your focus and get control of your emotions, especially if you don't like to travel or are an inexperienced traveler.

- How many days will you be gone?
- Which days are devoted exclusively to travel?
- What is the purpose of the trip (such as sightseeing, business, or a combination)
- What key events require a wardrobe change from the basic purpose of the trip?
- Will you see the same people every day?

Next, I have some tips to help you see exactly how you can travel with less. Every item in your suitcase should have a specific use. We want to cut down on those "just in case" items that clog up the process and the suitcase:

- Wear clothing more than once. Who will see you every day that you need to impress? Can you wear certain articles of clothing, such as a skirt, a pair of pants, or a blazer, more than once? If the people you see for a Friday meeting won't see you during your dinner with clients on Saturday, why not wear the same business suit? And if you see either of the same people on Monday, wear the same suit but change your accessories.
- Don't let toiletries weigh you down. If you are staying at a hotel or with friends and family, they likely have soap, hair care products, disposable razors, and a hair dryer. Can you comfortably leave these items at home? If you aren't sure what the hotel provides for guests, give them a call. Your suitcase just got lighter!
- Take advantage of laundry services or a dry cleaner. The hotel's laundry services will be costly, so check out

where the locals go. You could end up with fewer items to schlep in your suitcase if you're on an extended stay.

- Check the weather. You want to be prepared in case a heat wave or snowstorm suddenly appears on the Doppler radar. If the coast is clear, you can leave your heavy snow boots home while visiting family over Christmas.

This 8-minute round is now complete. Before you move on, do you want to make any notes?

Get Packing

Next, I want you to pretend that you're taking a trip so you can apply what you've just leaned to a real-world scenario. The following example is for women, but you can adapt the exercise for men or children. Suppose that you are getting ready for a four-day trip. You fly out on Thursday and return Sunday night. On Thursday, you will be having dinner with clients. On Friday, you will be in business meetings all day with another set of clients. On Saturday, you will be visiting with Aunt Roberta and Uncle Bertie, who insist that you spend the night and accompany them to a church service followed by brunch on Sunday. You fly home Sunday night.

Round One

On a sheet of paper, draw a box and write down the days you will be gone, as if you were writing on a week-at-a-glance calendar page. Take a few minutes to jot down what you would take on this fantasy trip (including what you will wear on the plane). When you're finished, I want you to compare it to my bare-bones but adequate list, which follows:

- One business suit
- One casual jacket/ blazer or coat (depending on the season)
- One pair jeans
- Two cashmere sweaters or one sleeveless and one short-sleeve (You'd make your decision based on the weather, type of activities, and so on)
- Two tee shirts (or one tee and one casual top)
- Four pair underpants
- Two bras
- Two pair socks; two pair nylons or tights
- One pair slipper socks
- One pair heels
- One pair flats
- One pair sneakers
- One small day purse
- One weekender travel bag
- Two scarves
- Two pair earrings
- Something lightweight to sleep in

Round Two

Consider the list you created in round one. How would these few items work over four days of business, travel, and family activities? I came up with the following:

THURSDAY	FRIDAY	SATURDAY	SUNDAY
(travel and dinner with clients)	(business meetings)	(family visit, dinner out)	(church, brunch, travel at night)
Travel: black business suit, first cashmere sweater (or short-sleeve top), black flats	*Business meetings:* black business suit, second cashmere sweater (or sleeveless top), black heels	*Family visit:* jeans, T-shirt, sneakers	*Church and brunch:* black business suit, first cashmere sweater or short-sleeve top, black heels
Dinner with clients: black business suit, first cashmere sweater (or short-sleeve top), black heels		*Dinner out:* with luck you can stay in your jeans and switch to a casual top. You can always punch up a jeans outfit with a nice scarf and a pair of heels.	*Casual time with relatives:* jeans, casual top, sneakers
Note: depending on the length of your flight, arrival time, and who meets you at the airport, you might travel in jeans, a casual top, and sneakers. Wear your blazer and a scarf on the plane. You could change into your suit at the hotel.			*Travel:* black business suit, first cashmere sweater (or short-sleeve top), black flats. You can travel home in your casual clothes, especially if you popped your jeans into the washer last night.

CLOTHING: Black or neutral-colored business suit for Thursday (suit color varies with the seasons).

Repeat business suit on Friday.

Wear suit on Sunday to church service.

SHOES: Black or beige flats for Thursday; can wear Saturday night out with family.

Black or beige heels for Friday and for Sunday service

Sneakers for the weekend's casual events.

One pair slipper socks for hotel room and relatives' home.

BIZ TOPS: Depending on the time of year, you might have two cashmere sweaters: one for the plane and one for your Friday meetings. Airports, planes, and offices tend to be chilly, so cashmere is a nice choice because it's lightweight and yet warm.

If the trip were during warm months, I'd have a short-sleeve top for travel days and a sleeveless one for Friday. If the buildings were chilly due to air conditioning, I could wear my jacket. If the buildings were warm, I'd be able to take off my jacket.

CASUAL TOPS/TEES: You could wear your travel outfit to church and brunch; change into jeans and a tee for time with relatives, and return to your original outfit for the flight home. A casual T-shirt would suffice if you were spending a day with family. Wear the casual top if you need to dress up those jeans for dinner or in case friends stop by. You could also leave these items home and wear your cashmere sweaters with your family.

ACCESSORIES: With one suit you can create multiple looks by changing not only the top but also your jewelry and scarf.

NIGHTTIME: One nightgown or a pair of PJs is plenty. Most hotels have robes and so will your family. "Borrow rather than schlep" are words to live by. Carry lightweight items to sleep in even if you're traveling in the dead of winter. After all, you will be able to control the temperature in your room so you won't be cold.

HANDBAG: A weekender is a bag that you can take on a plane as your second piece of luggage. (It has to fit under the seat in front of you.) I tuck my laptop in it and—voilà—I'm ready to work on the road or at my destination. Inside the weekender, I also have a small purse that I use for every day at my destination. The weekender also holds all my valuables—ID, cash, checks, and jewelry—as well as my cosmetics and a change of underwear. If I had to leave my suitcase, I'd be able to function. This minimalist approach will make you powerful and free.

PERSONAL CARE PRODUCTS: The TSA limits you to no more than a 3-ounce container for any liquid or gel product, and all containers must fit into a 1-quart bag. Either purchase the small size of your favorite products or create them by purchasing and filling small containers. Be sure you put labels on these containers so that the contents don't turn into mystery liquid. Prepping liquids can be more time consuming than packing your suitcase! I travel frequently, so I always have a cosmetics bag ready to go.

When I return from a trip, I replenish the containers. Trying sample products in hotels has introduced me to a few new favorites.

If you are moved to pack more for a trip, ask yourself why? Do you have a good reason or are you using "just in case" as an excuse? If you do need something, it is most likely available near your hotel or at a friend's or relative's home, unless you're headed to the Sahara or the Arctic. Consider the smallest common denominator for everything. (For example, pack two Band-Aids, not the entire box.)

Don't Forget the Essentials

Finally, a word to the wise about those few items you really can't do without. Be sure you have your prescription medications and vitamins counted out a few days in advance. If you wear contacts and glasses, make sure you always have both with you. If you wear one or the other, be sure you have a spare. The hotel may have shampoo but it won't have your prescriptions. Instead of thinking of things or stuff as your security, find your security in the freedom you gain when you have only one suitcase and an overnight bag. In the event of an emergency, you can drop your suitcase, knowing that your valuables are in the bag tossed over your shoulder. Now that's security!

Your New List Ritual

Knowing how to craft a list that is lean and to the point and that directs you to your goal—whether your goal is a productive day, a full pantry, a great trip, or any other endeavor—is a great skill to hone. You're working the Magic Formula here. Write down everything you can think of for any list and then

- Eliminate the excess
- Categorize items
- Organize those categories

And here's a bonus: Over time, you will get so skilled at making good lists that you will start the elimination process in your head. You begin to feel which items are not necessary to even consider. This skill may overwhelm some of you at the start, but work in short bursts of 8 minutes and you'll stay in control.

The goal of organizing is control: not a rigid hold on yourself, your environment, or those around you but a way to keep extraneous elements at bay so your energy is always focused on what you want to accomplish.

9
MAINTENANCE RITUALS (AND REWARDS)

No one could make a greater mistake than he who did nothing because he could only do a little.

—EDMUND BURKE

When I visit a certain friend, if I get up earlier than she does and want to take my morning coffee outside, I can't: The house alarm is on and I'm not allowed to have the code. These house rules drive me insane, but I must respect them—in the mind of my hostess, her house is more secure this way. Perhaps you visited a friend or a relative recently and had to quickly get clued in to the way the family does things?

Anything can become a ritual, from something incredibly silly to rituals handed down by families or entire cultures. For example, in most homes, the way people load a dishwasher is set in stone. (An entire scene in the movie

181

Rachel Getting Married was devoted to this very madness.) Maybe your best friend takes hours to do her laundry because she micromanages the sorting. We're a loyal species. I grew up in Brooklyn, and every Italian family I ever knew had a big family gathering on Sunday afternoon for a multicourse traditional meal. And you didn't tell Grandma you were too busy to attend.

Certain habits actually sabotage us. It's late at night and you are exhausted. The kids were cranky and uncooperative all day. You have an assignment due at work in the morning and have no idea how you're going to meet the deadline. But you make a late-night snack—even though you know you shouldn't eat at this hour—and settle down in front of the computer to do your work. The house is quiet. Suddenly you realize you haven't checked your e-mail and Facebook accounts since this morning, so you give yourself 15 minutes to peruse them and then get to work. An hour later, you are astonished when you look up and see the time! Even when we have no looming assignment, we often distract ourselves with late-night social media events and snacks. Never considered that a ritual, did you?

We tend to think of the rituals that keep a home clean and a household running smoothly as things that perfect people we read about in magazines do. Or we assume that morning and evening routines are only for those who were born organized. Maybe you've tried to create such routines in the past, but they never take hold and within two weeks the house is once again mired in chaos. Perhaps you're so convinced you can't do this that you are tempted to skip this chapter. But what if I told you that you *are* successful at creating routines, rules, and regulations for your home? The issue isn't their creation but their effectiveness.

Consider Your Rituals and Routines

Think about what you need to do around bedtime and in the morning. Those are peak activity periods when minutes can serve us or be squandered like chips in Vegas. I'd like you to take 8 minutes to examine your current routines and ask yourself one question about each: Does this hinder or help me? You're always free to create something new or different. Most chapters in this book have a routine for the specific area in question—exiting the kitchen (page 73), bathroom (page 75), family room, (page 122), bedroom (page 44), and kids' bedroom (page 155), as well as handling paper clutter (page 94). These routines are your templates. You can string any number of actions together and create a routine that saves you time and energy.

One caution: Although you should create rituals for every chaotic time period in the day, don't enforce them simultaneously. Too much change translates into upheaval and little good usually comes of those efforts. Choose a single routine to add and work it for three weeks before adding another one. Psychologists suggest that it takes 21 days to create a new habit. Tweak the routine as you go if necessary. When you move on to the next challenge, you'll have a sense of accomplishment. You can build on your success.

Extra Ammo

Routines can be brilliant and unenforceable at the same time if you don't take into account your body clock and the natural clocks of the folks with whom you share your life. What do I mean? Let's say you are a morning person. You love the dawn and do your best work as the sun appears. You create an incredible morning routine designed to get everyone out the door on time with all their needed gear and full tummies. The only problem? Your spouse is a night person. There's no way he or she can function successfully at dawn. Should you give up? No! Make a list of everything you'd like to see happen and then divide the tasks between those who rise early and the sleepyheads. The latter can make contributions in advance. Imagine how wonderful for the morning team to find the trash empty, the dishes clean, the table set, the fruit washed, and the laundry sorted. Your team uses the shower first, makes fresh coffee, and has a hot meal ready for the moon people when they stumble into the kitchen. Everyone is involved, but they work at different times and perform different tasks.

Schedule a Clean Routine

It takes planning and dedication to keep a home clean. And it doesn't seem to matter whether home is a tiny studio apartment or a 5,000-square-foot house in the heart of Beverly Hills. Perhaps the biggest culprit to avoid is the vague "I'll just do this later" vow. If we never wrap our minds around the details and create a schedule, we'll be flying blind. Here's a quick way to stay on top of things.

Schedule home cleaning chores over the course of a week. And I do mean schedule them on your calendar until they become a part of your routine, such as feeding Fido, making morning coffee, or checking your e-mail. Monday might be the perfect day for grocery shopping. Tuesday could be the day the laundry gets done. Dedicate Wednesday to deep cleaning all the bathrooms, and so on.

Scheduling tasks turns a potentially unpleasant job into simply something that needs to be done, such as brushing your teeth when you get out of bed. And because the scheduled task is an isolated issue on a given day, you won't get overwhelmed. You no longer walk into the bathroom (or kitchen, closet, or family room) wondering when you're going to find the time to clean it. You know exactly.

Take 8 minutes to craft a household cleaning chart for yourself and your family. A lot of discussion may be necessary before you can get the chart in motion, but with these 8 minutes you'll push the first domino. And although delegating is wonderful, keep in mind that your children need to be taught how to do tasks. Have your children perform the task with you or practice under your watchful eye. By mentoring your children, you also build their self-esteem—a great dividend.

Create a Bedtime Ritual

It seems like a thousand little things need to be done before the family can go to sleep. The number of tasks can be so overwhelming that we often run and seek solace in social media or the TV, the phone, a hobby, or food. Take 8 minutes to make a list of what habitually gets done around your home in the evening. Can you add anything that would make life easier? Can you remove anything from the list either by scheduling it for a different time of day or by assigning the task to another family member? Mothers often feel they do everything faster and better than anyone else in the family unit. That may be true, but you must be careful that you're not setting yourself up for exhaustion.

To help get your creative juices flowing, a mock list for the average family follows. Adjust it as you see fit:

- Shut off entertainment devices: TV, DVD player, video game console, and so on.
- Turn on the dishwasher (loaded right after dinner, thanks to your kitchen routine!).
- Check all the doors and windows to be sure they are locked.
- Set the table for breakfast to save time the next morning.
- Know the menu the night before and keep the weekday menu simple. You don't want to turn into a short-order cook when time is at a premium.
- If your children like cereal, keep it where they can reach it and serve themselves.
- Make lunches or at the very least do prep work such as chopping fruits and veggies for snacks. Nutritious doesn't have to be complicated.
- Check all backpacks. Have them ready to grab by the front door.

- Check homework and sign any school papers.
- Set the home alarm for security. (If you have an alarm, be sure you use it!)
- Set your alarm clock (an actual clock or the one on your cell phone).
- Select your outfit for the next day. Yes, even children should do this. If there's a glitch (you forgot something was in the laundry or at the cleaners or perhaps a button is missing), you have time to choose something else and can avoid a morning meltdown.

How would you tweak my list to create your nighttime ritual? No, you can't do this entire checklist in 8 minutes! But you can do it in segments that last 8 minutes or less each. Let's take a look:

- The first three items should take no time at all unless you live in a mansion and have a lot of territory to cover.
- The next four items are related to food. With older children helping, you can complete all four in 8 minutes.
- Checking backpacks will become a matter of rote as the school year rolls on. Remember, as your children get older, the idea of you even touching their backpack will be repugnant. Enjoy it while it lasts!
- Homework is up for grabs, isn't it? When children are young, homework is a breeze to check. When they are older, they don't need or want you to look at their assignments. The years in between is when the rubber hits the road and you have to bone up on certain subjects just to check your child's homework.

- I couldn't count the number of clients and friends I have who never set their home alarms. Get into the habit of making it the last detail you handle at night. Let everyone know the time it happens; you don't want it tripped by mistake. In many communities, any false report results in a fine. Don't forget to set your alarm clock as well.
- Now that everyone has an organized closet, setting out the outfit for the next day should take about 1 minute—maybe 3 minutes if you discover something is in the laundry or at the dry cleaners. Older children can certainly select their own outfits.

If your bedtime ritual has become too time consuming, try to steal 8-minute segments from another activity. The computer, television, reading, hobbies, and more all offer opportunities. You may feel deprived at first, but those activities will be waiting for you. Your child's career in school is fleeting and your time to contribute is relatively short.

It may also be necessary for your child to sacrifice an afterschool activity to start homework earlier in the evening. We keep kids on an endless cycle of activity these days without realizing that time to truly relax our bodies and our brains is equally important. See what kind of a compromise you can work out for the current semester.

Establish a Morning Ritual

The morning is going to run more smoothly if most of the work is done the night before. I know. I just said that, but it bears repeating. Who wants to wake up and find a stack of dirty dishes, that you have no clue what's for breakfast, or that your child's homework isn't correct? Best to face down these monsters in the dark, where they are more easily vanquished. Besides, taking care of these details the night before gives you a cushion of time in case something needs to be redone.

If the family members are all morning people, I suggest that you plan breakfast and check for ingredients and be sure homework is correct before you go to bed. You'll need to find something else for breakfast if you don't have what you need, and your child must have time to redo homework. The last minute in the morning is not the time to find out Johnny doesn't really know his times tables!

I presume that Mom is taking care of these details in the family, but if Dad is the early riser and the primary cook in the family, he will be in charge of the morning ritual. Sex doesn't determine who handles a chore: skill, interest, and practicality do. Is the following list reasonable for your family:

- Wake up and showers; the early riser then wakes up the next family member, and so on.
- Make breakfast.
- Make lunches (if not done the night before).
- Have a family member wash dishes or rinse and load the dishwasher.
- Dress, even if you're a stay-at-home mom. Wearing PJs at noon will have you feeling depressed.
- As you go out the door, check that the lights are off, windows and doors are shut and locked, you have

your keys, and the pets' water bowls are full of fresh water.

How close did I come to a morning schedule that would help your family? Families come in all sizes and shapes, and even people who live alone need a morning ritual. What does yours look like?

Reward Yourself

I have saved the best for last. When you do something you don't like or feel particularly unskilled at, give yourself a reward. Keep the reward and the task in perspective and you can't go wrong. You wouldn't give yourself a weekend at a spa just for doing the dishes! But you might celebrate the fact that this weekend the family pitched in, and the entire house was sparkling clean in no time at all. Here in no particular order are some of my favorite rewards. See what you would add to my list:

- Eat a piece of high-quality chocolate.
- Enjoy a drink at your favorite coffee shop.
- Purchase a book you've wanted to read.
- Make a phone call to a friend or relative who lives far away.
- Luxuriate in a long bubble bath.
- Take in a movie with a friend.
- Dance to a new music album.
- Go outside and play with the dog.

What would be on your list? The hardest thing for just about all of my clients is embracing the reward concept. I usually hear that no reward is due for something "I should have done." Really? No reward is due, but punishment gets meted out without a thought in terms of guilt? Put an end to this cycle. Guilt serves no purpose. If you haven't been organized or kept a clean house, you can start today. And instead of entertaining guilt, why not peruse the past and find out what held you back? This type of exploration is not easy but will be empowering.

You've heard the old saying "it's better to teach a man how to grow potatoes than it is to give him a few." This chapter is meant to inspire you to think in terms of connections, partnerships, and eliminations and to grow your own unique solutions. What tasks can logically be done in sequence? To whom can I delegate a task? And what activity can I shorten or eliminate to have more time for something that's important right now? With the time you devote to a few short routines, you'll reap a home environment of increased peace and order.

Practice, Practice, Practice

I had a friend whose mother made him take piano lessons when he was a child. At first he hated to practice but persevered because his teacher insisted; she sensed he had a gift. Time passed and one day something amazing happened: Ron suddenly enjoyed playing the piano. He easily excelled at all types of music. He discovered this talent not only attracted girls but also opened doors that might otherwise not be open to him. As he became older and continued to practice, he learned that he had other musical talents—he could write lyrics and compose music. He has since won multiple Emmy awards composing music and lyrics for many TV programs. None of it would have happened if his teacher hadn't insisted that he stick with it.

Organizing is a skill to practice like any other. My final words of wisdom are to stick with it!—even if for just 8 dedicated minutes. A little bit of organization may take you a long way.

In terms of our enjoying a happy day-to-day existence,
the calmer our minds are, the greater our peace of mind
will be and the greater will be our ability to enjoy
a happy and joyful life.
—DALAI LAMA

APPENDIX A: ORGANIZING TOOLS

BEDROOM

Brackets and a shelf

Canvas garment covers

Clear sweater drawer

Drawer organizers for socks, bras, and underwear

Hamper

Jewelry box, cork, and/or acrylic jewelry holder

Shelf creator

Shelf dividers

Small bookcase

Trash can

FlipFOLD laundry folder

Lined basket or clear storage drawers for socks (same as the ones used for sweaters or shoes)

Over-the-door canvas shoe rack

Wooden shoe rack or clear shoe drawers

Wooden or Slip Grip–style hangers

KITCHEN

Airtight glass food containers

Boot tray

Cooler for the car

Corner Organizer Rack

Drawer liner

Drawer organizers for cooking and baking tools

Fire extinguisher

Foldable two-step step stool

Grid totes for the pantry and under the sink

Heavy-duty rubber-type container for cleaning products

Junk drawer organizer

Knife sharpener

Lid storage

Padded china storage containers

Pet food and pet treat containers

Portable shelves

Shelf creator for canned goods

Shelf dividers for the pantry

Spice rack

Zippered plastic bags in assorted sizes

BATHROOM

Acrylic makeup holders for the countertop

Baker's rack

Drawer liners

Drawer organizers

Grid totes

Grid totes for first aid supplies, hair care products

Hooks and extra bars

Over-the-tub portable shelf

Portable shelf for linen closet

Shower caddy or grid tote

Space-saver over-toilet storage unit
Tub pillow

HOME OFFICE/
PAPER CLUTTER MANAGEMENT

Baskets for magazines and newspapers
Basket for mail
Calendar
Hanging file folders
Hanging file folder with 2-inch-wide box-bottom
Holder for magazines or catalogs
Label maker with extra cassettes
Manila folders
Portable file box in wicker or (faux) leather
Portable file caddy
Shredder (cross cut)
Storage boxes

FAMILY ROOM

Acid-free paper and archival quality boxes for photo
    storage and/or memorabilia
Basket for newspapers
Basket or holder for magazines
Basket for remotes
Bin, chest, and/or pop-up container for toys
CD storage: bookcase, built-in drawers, music holders,
    binders and sleeves; or digital storage solutions (iPod,
    iCloud, iTunes, exterior hard drive, and so on)
Containers for craft supplies

Energy-saving light bulbs
Zippered storage bags for game pieces

KIDS' ROOMS

Bins for toys
Camera and printer for printing photo labels
Containers for backpack
Container for savings bank
Drawer liners and drawer organizers for kids' bathroom
DVD and video game storage: bookcase, built-in drawers, holders, binders and sleeves
Grid totes
Hangers (same as adult for older children)
Hanging canvas sweater or shoe bag (with multiple compartments) for toys or clothing
Homework storage: colored folders; hole punch or sheet protectors or project boxes; large binders; subject tabs for binders
Low-hanging closet bar
One-step step stool
Over-the-door canvas shoe bag for small toys
Tubular child-size hangers for small-size clothing and one or two padded hangers for special outfits
Zippered storage bags for small toys and game pieces

APPENDIX B: RESOURCES

DONATIONS

Clothing and Household Items

Career Gear
  www.careergear.org
  Provides professional attire for job interviews to
    disadvantaged men

Dress for Success
  www.dressforsuccess.org
  Provides professional attire for job interviews to
    disadvantaged women

Goodwill Industries International
  www.goodwill.org
  Sells clothing and household goods

One Warm Coat
  www.onewarmcoat.org
  Collects and distributes coats for free to those in need

Salvation Army
  www.salvationarmy.com
  Sells clothing and household goods

Computer Technology

The following sites refurbish and distribute computer technology (laptops, desktops, printers) to economically disadvantaged youths in the United States and around the world.

Computers 4 Kids
  www.c4k.org

National Cristina Foundation
  www.cristina.org

World Computer Exchange
  www.worldcomputerexchange.org

Miscellaneous Items

Give the Gift of Sight
  www.givethegiftofsight.com
  Provides free prescription eyewear to individuals in
    North America and developing countries around
    the world. Drop off eyeglasses or sunglasses at
    LensCrafters, Pearle Vision, Sears Optical, Target
    Optical, BJ's Optical, Sunglass Hut, or Lions Club.

Hungry for Music
  www.hungryformusic.org
  Distributes used musical instruments to
    underprivileged children

Luggage
  www.suitcasesforkids.org
  Provides luggage for foster children who move from
    home to home

Reader to Reader
www.readertoreader.org
Accepts books for children and teens and distributes
to school libraries nationwide

MEMORABILIA, PHOTOGRAPHS, AND SCRAPBOOKING SUPPLIES

Supplies and Ideas

Creating Keepsakes
www.creatingkeepsakes.com
Website of the *Creating Keepsakes Scrapbook*
magazine

Creative Memories
www.creativememories.com
Provides scrapbook ideas and supplies

Exposures
www.exposuresonline.com
Offers albums and scrapbooks

Scrapbooking 101
www.scrapbooking101.com
Your guide to the basics of scrapbooking

Online Photo Management and Sharing

Flickr
www.flickr.com

Picasa (from Google)
http://picasa.google.com

Shutterfly
www.shutterfly.com

Snapfish (a division of Hewlett-Packard)
www.snapfish.com

MIND, BODY, AND SPIRIT

Mysteries.Net
www.mysteries.net
Meditation and yoga site

Self-Realization Fellowship
www.selfrealizationfellowship.org
Meditation and yoga site

Transcendental Meditation
www.TM.org
Meditation and yoga site

NATURAL CLEANING

About.com (managed by the *New York Times*)
http://housekeeping.about.com/cs/environment/a/
alternateclean.htm

Meyer's Clean Day
www.mrsmeyers.com

Seventh Generation Products
www.seventhgeneration.com

OFFICE AND FILING SUPPLIES

Day Runner
www.DayRunner.com

Office Depot
www.officedepot.com

OfficeMax
www.officemax.com

Fitter
www.fitter1.com
Fitter Active Sitting Disc transforms your chair. Check
out other ergonomically correct products.

Levenger
www.Levenger.com
Binders, calendars, magazine holders, and more.

Staples
www.staples.com

ONLINE AUCTION AND SALE SITES

eBay
www.ebay.com

Cash for CDs
www.cashforcds.com

Craig's List
www.craigslist.com

RECYCLE

1-800-GOT-JUNK?
   www.1800gotjunk.com or call 1-800-468-5865
   Removes just about anything (furniture, appliances, electronics, yard waste, and renovation debris) and makes every effort to recycle or donate items

Rechargeable Battery Recycling Corporation (RBRC)
   www.call2recycle.org or call 1-877-273-2925
   Recycles used portable rechargeable batteries and old cell phones

REDUCE AND STOP UNWANTED MAIL

Opt-Out of Preapproved Credit Card
and Insurance Offers
   www.optoutprescreen.com or call 1-888-567-8688
   Official website of the Credit Reporting Industry to accept and process consumer requests to opt-in or opt-out of prescreened credit card and insurance offers

Direct Marking Association (DMA)
   www.the-dma.org
   Reduces your total volume of mail when you register for the Direct Marketing Association's Mail Preference Service (MPS)

SHOP

Bed Bath & Beyond
   www.bedbathandbeyond.com

Michael's Arts & Crafts
  www.michaels.com

The Container Store
  www.thecontainerstore.com

THE AUTHOR

Regina Leeds

www.ReginaLeeds.com
  Facebook: Regina Leeds, The Zen Organizer
  Twitter: The Zen Organizer
  E-mail: ZenOrg1@aol.com

ACKNOWLEDGMENTS

I find one vast garden spread out all over the universe.
All plants, all human beings, all higher mind bodies
are about in this garden in various ways, each has
his own uniqueness and beauty. Their presence and variety
give me great delight. Every one of you adds with his
special feature to the glory of the garden.
—SRI ANANANDAMAYI MA

To everyone at Perseus Publishing I extend my deepest thanks. You have given me the literary home every writer dreams of having.

To my editor extraordinaire, Katie McHugh, I dedicate these song lyrics: "You're simply the best—better than all the rest." Indeed you are, Katie. Indeed you are. This is our fifth time out and I'm already looking forward to the next one.

To the tireless Christine Marra of *Marra*thon Production Services and her band of merry cohorts—copy editor Susan Pink, designer and typesetter Jane Raese, proofreader Josephine Mariea, and indexer Donna Riggs—I pledge my undying gratitude for a job well done. No one outside the publishing world understands the complicated process a book goes through on its journey from writer's hands to printing press. You do the impossible: You make it fun. I feel safe with you.

To Christina Hernandez, a gifted artist and dear friend, I say thank you for gracing this book with your illustrations. You are that rare woman who is as beautiful on the inside as she is on the outside. And that beauty is reflected in your work.

To my literary agent, Marilyn Allen, I send bouquets of thanks for believing in me and understanding the possibility of Zen Organizing when no one else did and for co-creating the journey with me.

To my friends who have endured the trials of an artist's life with me I say thank you from the bottom of my heart. We laugh. We cry. We do life together. You have all taught me the meaning of family. The bond we share is thicker than blood.

And finally I send a special hug into the cosmos for my beloved friend Wayne Allwine. We all miss you, Buddy. I've got my eye on Russi. Till we meet again ~

Regina Leeds
Los Angeles
January 2012

INDEX

"Ambitious 8's"
description, xviii
See also specific rooms
Aromatherapy, 92

Backpacks, 148–149, 187
Banking tips, 103, 105–106,
114
"Bargains"/sales, 72, 88,
107
"Basic 8's"
description, xviii
See also specific rooms
Bathroom
"ambitious 8's," 86–92
"basic 8's," 82–85
cosmetics shelf life, 77–
78
exit ritual, 75–76
"Extra Ammo," 77–78
fresh eyes exercise, 78–
79
hair products, 86–89

hamper, 81
lighting, 92
medicines/first aid items,
80–81, 82–83
paper product storage, 84
"quickies," 80–82
reading material in, 82
shower caddy, 87
speed elimination, 79–80
supply kits, 85
towels and, 81–82
trash basket, 81
under the sink, 91–92
Bathroom monitor, 85
Bed Bath & Beyond, 130
Bed-making
adults, 7, 20
children, 142, 149
Bedroom
"ambitious 8's," 34–43
"basic 8's," 27–34
books/bookcases, 28–29,
28 (fig.)

Bedroom (*continued*)
  drawer organizers, 34
    (fig.)
  dresser drawers/
    organizers, 34 (fig),
    35–36
  entry/exit rituals, 44–45
  "Extra Ammo," 20–21
  fresh eyes exercise,
    21–22
  hampers, 25–26
  jewelry, 41–43
  lighting, 26
  maintaining
    organization, 44–45
  nightstands/drawers,
    33–34
  organizing overview,
    19–45
  "quickies" tasks, 23–26
  scheduling large tasks,
    21–22
  speed elimination, 22–23,
    38
  "stray" clothing, 28
  toys (children/pets),
    31–33
  trashcan, 26
  under the bed, 40–41
  See also Child's room;
    Clothing

Bedroom closets
  dry cleaner plastic,
    23–24
  grouping/arranging
    clothing, 37
  handbags, 27
  hangers, 24–25
  shelves/additional
    shelves, 29
  shoes, 37–39
  sweaters, 30–31
  thinning out clothes,
    36–37
  See also Clothing
Bedroom floor, 31–33
Bedtime routine, 185–188
Boethius, 121
Briefcase, 106–107
Burke, Edmund, 181

Calendars
  bill paying, 114–115
  "bird's eye view" with,
    160–161
  changes and, 160, 165
  family connecting, 105
  habit with, 95, 99–100
  home cleaning chores
    and, 185
  medical/vet
    appointments, 104

requests for your time and, 164

to-do lists and, 159–160, 164–166

types, 99–100, 105, 159–160

Catalogs, 110–111

Categorize (step), xiv

Cather, Willa, 19

CDs/music, 132–134

Change
reactions to, xi–xii
too much change and, 183

Change preparation
goals and, 2–4
habits and, 7–9
health and, 5–6
overcoming difficulties, 4–6
questions on your past, 1–2

Children's artwork, 139–140

Child's bathroom, 151–152

Child's homework
area for, 153–154
organizing, 154
parent checking, 187, 189
parent/child working together, 155

Child's room
"ambitious 8's," 150–154
backpacks, 148–149
"basic 8's," 148–150
bed-making/linens, 142, 149
child's input, 144
cleanup tips, 149–150
closets, 146–148
clothing, 147–148, 150, 151
earning/saving money, 148
"Extra Ammo," 143
fresh eyes exercise, 143–145
habits for children, 142–143
hangers, 146–147, 151
model for, 141, 156
outgrown items, 143–144
photo labels, 147–148
"quickies," 146–148
ritual with, 155
speed elimination, 145
toy organization/organizers, 146 (fig.), 150

Chinmoy, Sri, 47

Chödrön, Pema, 141

Cleaning routine, 184–185

Clothing
  child's room, 147–148, 150, 151
  cotton covers for, 24
  daily habits with, 7–8
  emotional attachment and, 20–21
  hangers for, 24–25, 146–147, 151
  traveling tips, 172–173, 174–177
  See also Bedroom; Bedroom closets
Color order, 27, 37
Completion habit, 8, 48–49
Container Store, 24, 29, 31, 59, 81, 95, 133, 139
Cooler storage, 55–56
Cosmetics. *See* Makeup
Costco, 27, 72, 84
Credit score, 100

Da Vinci, Leonardo, 93
Dalai Lama, 157, 192
Dishes/habits, 8
Dream board, 4
Dry cleaner plastic, 23–24, 146
DVDs, 134

Edison, Thomas, 75

8-minute organizing
  "ambitious 8's" term, xviii
  "basic 8's" term, xviii
  finding time, xvii–xviii
  "quickies" term, xviii
  who can benefit from, xv–xvii
Eliminate (step), xiv
Exercise, 6
Exit rituals
  bathroom, 75–76
  bedroom, 44–45
  family room, 122
  kitchen, 73–74
Expirations/dates
  hair products, 88
  makeup, 77–78
  meat storage guidelines, 69
  prescriptions/medicines, 80–81, 83
"Extra Ammo" actions
  description, 9
  paper organization, 100
  rituals/routines, 184
  See also specific rooms

"Fake prosperity," 59
Family room
  "ambitious 8's," 131–140

assigning chores, 123–124

"basic 8's," 127–131

children's artwork, 139–140

docking station, 126

DVDs, 134

e-reading and, 135

exit ritual, 122

"Extra Ammo," 123–124

fresh eyes exercise, 124

hobbies, 136–138

lighting, 125, 126–127

moving furniture, 131

music/CDs, 132–134

paper clutter, 130–131

photos in, 138–139

"quickies," 125–127

reading room creation, 134–136

remotes, 125–126

speed elimination, 125

taking pictures, 127

toys, 127–130, 129 (fig), 130 (fig.)

vacuuming, 126

FICO credit score, 100

File system

action files, 93–94, 95, 97, 98, 103, 104, 115

archives, 115–116

benefits, 93–94

income tax receipts/returns, 106, 111–112, 115, 116

mail, 95–98

pending folders, 61, 97, 98, 104, 112, 115

receipts to retain, 111–114

warranties/instruction manuals, 116–117

Fire extinguisher, 72

Fireproof metal box, 106

FlipFOLD laundry folder, 31

Fragrances, 92

Free Cycle, 135

Fresh eyes exercise

description, 15, 16

to-do lists, 161–162

See also specific rooms

"Game Saver" boxes, 129

Gandhi, 141

Garcia, Sarah, 77

Goodwill, 53, 135

Gregory the Great, St., ix

Grid totes, 65, 67, 71, 81, 83, 87, 88, 90, 91, 136, 152

Habits
  bed-making, 7, 20, 142
  calendar and, 99–100
  children/their room,
    142–143
  completing actions, 8,
    48–49
  daily examples, 7–8
  establishment time, 8,
    183
  "invitation by example,"
    8–9
  minor tasks and, 158–159
  overview, 7–9
  positive affirmation, 123
  recycling/trash, 7
  to-do lists and, 165–166
  See also Rituals/routines
Hampers, 25–26, 81
Handbags
  organizing, 27
  traveling and, 177
Hangers for clothing, 24–
  25, 146–147, 151
Health
  medicines/first aid items,
    80–81, 82–83
  positive affirmation, 123
  rewards and, 190–191
  scheduling medical/vet
    appointments, 104

  tips, 5–6, 82
  trips/packing and, 178
  See also Expirations/
    dates; Meditation
Hemorrhoids, 82
Hobbies, 118–119, 136–138
Home alarms, 181, 187,
  188
Home office
  as combo room, 101
  fresh eyes exercise,
    100–102
  hobbies/supplies and,
    137
  speed elimination,
    102–103
  supplies, 107
  See also Paper
    organization
Homework. *See* Child's
  homework

Identity theft prevention,
  50
Ikea, 29, 55
Incremental organizing
  steps, x
  See also 8-minute
    organizing
Instruction manuals/
  warranties, 116–117

Jewelry
  insurance and, 43
  organizing jewelry, 41–43
Jouer Cosmetics, 77
Jung, Carl, 1
Junk drawer/organizer,
  64–65

Keys' placement/habit, 7, 8
Kitchen
  "ambitious 8's," 62–72
  "basic 8's," 56–62
  broken equipment,
    52–53
  children's cabinet
    section, 54
  china storage, 62–63
  cleaning as you go, 53
  completion habit, 48–49
  cooking/baking tools, 58
  countertop appliances,
    63–64
  everyday
    dishes/glassware, 55,
    55 (fig.)
  exit ritual, 73–74
  "Extra Ammo," 49
  fresh eyes exercise,
    49–50
  junk drawer/organizer,
    64–65

leftover containers,
  58–60
lid organizers, 59, 59
  (fig.)
lighting, 74
linens/pot holders, 52
mystery/multiple tools,
  57–58
pantry, 65–68
pantry moth prevention,
  49
pet food organization,
  54–55, 54 (fig.)
"quickies," 52–56
speed elimination
  papers, 50–51
spices/herbs, 56–57
step stool, 53
storage ideas, 67–68
under the sink, 70–72
utensils holder, 55
Kitchen/refrigerator
  front/outside, 60–62
  inside, 68–70
  meat storage guidelines,
    69
Knife sharpening, 57

Life tweaks. See Habits
Lighting
  bathroom, 92

Lighting (*continued*)
  bedroom, 26
  energy-saving bulbs, 127
  family room, 125, 126–127
  kitchen, 74
Linen closet, 81–82, 83
List making
  overview, 157–158
  packing lists, 171–178
  ritual with, 179
  shopping lists, 166–168, 169–170 (fig.)
  See also To-do lists

Magazine holders, 109, 109 (fig.), 111, 130
Magazines, 108–110, 111
Magic Formula, xiii–xiv, 179
Mail basket, 95, 95 (fig.)
Mail organizing
  filing system, 95
  overview, 95–99
Maintenance. *See* Rituals/routines
Makeup
  expiration dates, 77–78
  organizing, 89–91
  traveling and, 177–178
Makeup organizer, 90
Marcos, Imelda, 37

Meat storage guidelines, 69
Meditation
  benefits, 12
  one-pointed mind and, 12–13
  technique description, 12–13
Michael's, 64
Mind map, 4
Morning routine, 188–190
Mudroom creation, 56
Multitasking
  about, 12, 13
  one-pointed mind vs., 11–12, 13–14
Music/CDs, 132–134

Nightstands
  organizing drawers, 33–34
  power and, 33

One-pointed mind
  description, 11–12
  meditation and, 12–13
  multitasking vs., 11–12, 13–14
One Year to an Organized Life (Leeds), 77
One Year to . . . series (Leeds), xv, 2, 15, 77

Online bill paying, 106, 114

Organize (step), xiv

Organizing
actions summary, 157
change and, xi–xii
control and, 179
description, 17–18
practice and, 191–192
storing items on sides, 70, 129, 129 (fig.)
tidying vs., 17
See also 8-minute organizing; Zen organizing; *specific components*; *specific rooms*

"Organizing fever," 9

Organizing products
advice on purchasing, 14–15
organizing vs., 15
See also specific products

Packing lists
essentials, 178
exercise/example on, 173–177
overview, 171–178
personal care products, 177–178
questions to answer, 171–172
tips on traveling with less, 172–173
weather and, 173
weekender bag, 177

Pantry, 49, 65–68

Paper Back Swap, 135

Paper organization
"ambitious 8's," 108–119
banking and, 103, 105–106, 114
"basic 8's," 105–108
briefcase, 106–107
calendar and, 95, 99
canceling subscriptions, 108, 110, 111
catalogs, 110–111
direct deposit, 103
"Extra Ammo," 100
family room, 130–131
hobbies/special interests, 118–119, 137
income tax receipts/returns, 106, 111–112, 115, 116
magazines, 108–110, 111
mail handling, 95–99
office supplies, 107
paying bills, 114–115
"quickies," 103–105

Paper organization
(*continued*)
receipts to retain,
111–114
ritual with, 94–99
shredding/shredder and,
104–105
speed elimination, 50–51
See also File system;
Home office
"Penny wise but pound
foolish," 72, 88, 107
Photo labels, 147–148
"Piggy banks," 110, 148
Poisons under the kitchen
sink, 70, 71
Positive affirmation, 123
Prescriptions/medicines
expiration dates, 80–81,
83
handling old
prescriptions, 80
trips/packing and, 178

"Quickies" tasks
benefits from, 23
description, xviii
See also specific rooms

Rachel Getting Married
(movie), 181–182

Reading room creation,
134–136
Refrigerator. *See* Kitchen/
refrigerator
Remotes, 125–126
Rewarding yourself, 190–
191
Rituals/routines
bedtime, 185–188
child's room, 155
cleaning routine,
184–185
dishwasher loading
example, 181–182
establishment of, 181–
182
"Extra Ammo," 184
list making, 179
morning people/night
people and, 184
mornings, 188–190
overview, 181–183
paper organization, 94–
99
too much change and,
183
See also Exit rituals
Roosevelt, Eleanor, xix
Routines. *See*
Rituals/routines
Russell, Tanya, 49, 58

Scrapbooking, 136

Second guessing yourself, 51

Secondhand stores, 29

Self-directed life and time, 10–11

Shelf life. *See* Expirations/dates

Shelves
adding in bedroom closets, 29
corner shelf unit, 55, 55 (fig.)
shelf creators, 54, 54 (fig.), 67–68, 83

Shoes/shoe racks, 39

Shopping lists
examples, 167–168, 169–170 (fig.)
online examples, 167
overview, 166–168, 169–170 (fig.)

Shredding paper/shredder, 104–105

Sisyphus, ix–x

Sleep needs, 6

Social media and time, 10, 182

Socks
organizer for, 36
storing tips, 35–36

Speed elimination
description, 15, 16–17
paper organization, 50–51
to-do lists, 162–163
"trash muscle" and, 22–23
See also specific rooms

Spice rack, 57

Step stool, 53

Subscriptions, 108, 110, 111

Sweaters
moths and, 31
organizing, 30–31

Time
movement vs. productivity, 161
requests for your time, 10–11, 164
self-directed life and, 10–11
social media and, 10, 182
using downtime between activities, 13–14, 53
See also One-pointed mind

To-do lists
calendar and, 159–160, 164–166
delegation and, 163–164

To-do lists (*continued*)
  fresh eyes exercise, 161–162
  judgment and, 161–162
  overview, 159
  scheduling habit and, 165–166
  speed elimination, 162–163
Toys organization
  board games, 129, 129 (fig.)
  child's room, 146, 146 (fig.), 150
  family room, 127–130, 129 (fig), 130 (fig.)
  "Game Saver" boxes, 129

  parent's bedroom and, 31–33
  stuffed toys, 129–130, 130 (fig.)
Trip lists. *See* Packing lists

Warranties/instruction manuals, 116–117
Water consumption needs, 6

Zen organizing
  description, xii–xiii, 17–18
  origins of term, xii–xiii
  See also Magic Formula
Zen proverb, 48–49